# PCs
## FOR
# DUMMIES®
## QUICK REFERENCE
### 3RD EDITION

D1072325

# PCs

## FOR

# DUMMIES®

## QUICK REFERENCE

### 3RD EDITION

## by Dan Gookin

**WILEY**

Wiley Publishing, Inc.

**PCs For Dummies® Quick Reference, 3rd Edition**

Published by
**Wiley Publishing, Inc.**
111 River Street
Hoboken, NJ 07030-5774

Copyright © 2005 by Wiley Publishing, Inc., Indianapolis, Indiana

Published by Wiley Publishing, Inc., Indianapolis, Indiana

Published simultaneously in Canada

For general information on our other products and services, please contact our Customer Care Department within the U.S. at 800-762-2974, outside the U.S. at 317-572-3993, or fax 317-572-4002.

For technical support, please visit www.wiley.com/techsupport.

Wiley also publishes its books in a variety of electronic formats. Some content that appears in print may not be available in electronic books.

Library of Congress Control Number: 2005923221

ISBN-13: 978-0-7645-8960-7

ISBN-10: 0-7645-8960-1

Manufactured in the United States of America

10 9 8 7 6 5 4 3 2 1

3O/QU/QU/QV/IN

WILEY

# About the Author

**Dan Gookin** has been writing about technology for 20 years. He has contributed articles to numerous high-tech magazines and written more than 100 books about personal computing technology, many of them accurate.

He combines his love of writing with his interest in technology to create books that are informative and entertaining, but not boring. Having sold more than 14 million copies translated into more than 30 languages, Dan can attest that his method of crafting computer tomes does seem to work.

Perhaps Dan's most famous title is the original *DOS For Dummies,* published in 1991. It became the world's fastest-selling computer book, at one time moving more copies per week than the *New York Times* number-one best seller (although, because it's a reference book, it could not be listed on the *NYT* best seller list). That book spawned the entire line of *For Dummies* books, which remains a publishing phenomenon to this day.

Dan's most recent titles include *Troubleshooting Your PC For Dummies,* 2nd Edition; *C All-in-One Desk Reference For Dummies; PCs For Dummies,* 9th Edition; *Buying a Computer For Dummies,* 2005 Edition; *Dan Gookin's Naked Windows XP;* and *Dan Gookin's Naked Office.* He also publishes a free weekly computer newsletter, "Weekly Wambooli Salad," full of tips, how-tos, and computer news, and he maintains the vast and helpful Web page www.wambooli.com.

Dan holds a degree in communications and visual arts from the University of California, San Diego. He lives in the Pacific Northwest, where he enjoys spending time with his four boys in the gentle woods of Idaho.

# Publisher's Acknowledgments

We're proud of this book; please send us your comments through our online registration form located at www.dummies.com/register/.

Some of the people who helped bring this book to market include the following:

### Acquisitions, Editorial, and Media Development

**Project Editor:** Rebecca Whitney

**Acquisitions Editor:** Greg Croy

**Technical Editor:** James F. Kelly

**Editorial Manager:** Carol Sheehan

**Media Development Supervisor:** Richard Graves

**Editorial Assistant:** Amanda Foxworth

### Production

**Project Coordinator:** Adrienne Martinez

**Layout and Graphics:** Brian Drumm, Lauren Goddard, Stephanie D. Jumper, Lynsey Osborn, Mary Gillot Virgin

**Proofreaders:** Laura Albert, Laura L. Bowman, Leeann Harney

**Indexer:** TECHBOOKS Production Services

---

**Publishing and Editorial for Technology Dummies**

**Richard Swadley,** Vice President and Executive Group Publisher

**Andy Cummings,** Vice President and Publisher

**Mary Bednarek,** Executive Acquisitions Director

**Mary C. Corder,** Editorial Director

**Publishing for Consumer Dummies**

**Diane Graves Steele,** Vice President and Publisher

**Joyce Pepple,** Acquisitions Director

**Composition Services**

**Gerry Fahey,** Vice President of Production Services

**Debbie Stailey,** Director of Composition Services

# Contents at a Glance

# Table of Contents

# The Personal Computer

In the 1960s, you could stun guests in your home with a color television set, but they would experience apoplexy at the sight of a computer there. Even in the 1980s, the appearance of a home computer was often met with a head-shaking "Whatever" by anyone you tried to impress. Yes, at one time, it was easy to pluck the PC out of the big picture. It was unusual. It was unexpected.

Today, the PC is as much a part of the big picture as a paper shredder in a law office. Yet, despite its ubiquity, the PC maintains an air of mystery and the scent of fear.

In this part, I pull together the pieces parts of a PC and give you a visual tour, some basic understanding, and some examples of what a computer can do. It's your preview of coming attractions to a device that's useful, fun, and even (dare I say?) friendly.

## In this part . . .

- ✓ What You See
- ✓ I/O Symbol Table
- ✓ The Basics

# What You See: Basic Hardware

A computer isn't really a single thing. It's a collection of things all clustered together and connected by various ugly cables. Each of these separate components makes up your computer system.

The central item in the computer system is the *console*, which is the main box that just about everything else plugs into. Other items surrounding the console are referred to as *peripherals*. Some are required, some are optional. There's enough variety and potential so that just about every computer system can be unique, customized for the needs of each computer owner.

Though the computer system you have, or may be looking at, is unique to you, all computer systems have a basic set of peripherals and options attached, as illustrated in the nearby figures. Here are the basic components you should recognize and know by their official names:

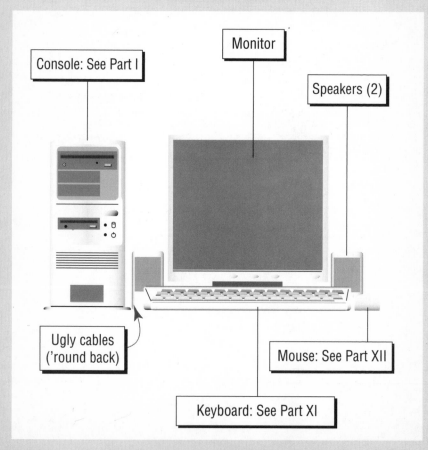

Console: See Part I

Monitor

Speakers (2)

Ugly cables ('round back)

Mouse: See Part XII

Keyboard: See Part XI

✔ **Console:** The centerpiece of any computer system, which houses the main circuitry board, microprocessor, memory (RAM), disk drives, plus lots of connectors for everything else. It's the box-o-guts! Also called the *system unit* and often mistakenly referred to as the *CPU*. See also Part I.

✔ **Monitor:** The computer's display. It can sit on top of or to the side of the console. This part of the basic computer system is necessary because it's how you see the information the computer displays.

✔ **Keyboard:** The thing you type on, and one method for you to send information to the computer. Despite all its graphics, most of the time you spend using the computer involves typing. See also Part XI.

✔ **Mouse:** The gizmo that helps you work with graphical images that the computer displays on the screen. It's the second method you use for entering information (next to the keyboard). See also Part XII.

✔ **Speakers:** The PC speaks! And squawks, and plays music, and often talks. To hear that stuff, you need speakers. These can be either external or part of the monitor. See also Part I.

✔ **Printer:** The device that puts your work down on paper — documents, copies of e-mail messages, charts, graphics, photos, or anything else your creative heart desires. See also Part VIII.

✔ **Lots of ugly cables:** Rarely seen in the showroom and never in ads, although they exist! Cables! Lots of ugly cables keep everything connected. They're usually found 'round back of the console and other components. Yes, even on wireless systems, there are still lots of cables. See also Part I.

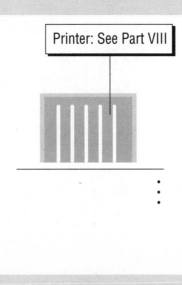

Printer: See Part VIII

A computer system can include a variety of other devices and gizmos beyond the basic items mentioned here. These *peripherals* include scanners, digital cameras, external disk drives, modems, and a host of other gadgets various and sundry.

## What You See: Console — the Front

The console is the star in your computer's solar system, the central hub of activity. Every other device, gizmo, or gadget in the computer system plugs into the console in one way or another. The console is also home to many of your PC's most important parts.

The illustration shows important items on the front side of the console. These are things you should be able to locate and identify on your own computer, though their specific locations may be different from what you see here.

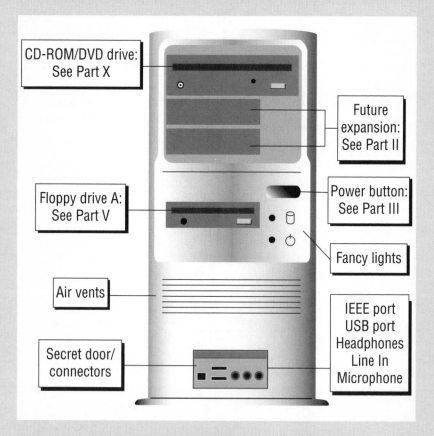

✔ **CD-ROM or DVD drive:** This is one of your computer's disk drives, designed for CD or DVD disks. Note that you may have more than one of these drives, such as both a CD and DVD drive. The drive may also be hidden behind a panel or door.

✔ **Future expansion:** You can add additional disk drives or devices to the console. They may be obvious or well-hidden by using the console's design.

✔ **Floppy drive:** Not every PC sold today has a floppy drive, but if yours does, it appears somewhere on the front of the console. This drive is designed to accept floppy disks.

✔ **Air vents:** The thing's gotta breathe!

✔ **Secret door/connectors:** Many consoles have special connectors on the front for USB devices, digital video (IEEE 1394), and audio connectors. These may be obvious on the front of the console or hidden behind a door or panel, or they may not exist at all.

✔ **Buttons and lights:** The console has at least one button and some lights. Additional buttons may appear on some consoles, as with additional lights. The following list highlights some of the more common buttons and lights:

- **Power button:** This button is used to start up the computer, turn the computer off, or do any of a number of other things. See also Part III.

- **Reset button:** This button lets you take control during times of woe, by essentially forcing the computer to stop and start in one swift punch. It's a powerful button, though not every console has one.

- **Sleep button:** This button appears mostly on laptop PCs and is used to put the system into a special sleep, or Stand By, mode. Few consoles have such a button, yet the sleep icon may appear as a light on the console, to indicate that the computer is not off, but, rather, "asleep."

- **Hard drive light:** This light flashes as the hard drive is being accessed. Because hard drives are often buried internally, the light provides a visual clue to whether the drive is alive or dead.

- **Power light:** This is merely a light on the console that is on when the computer is on. If your computer doesn't make much noise, this light is often your only clue that the sucker is turned on.

This list doesn't cover everything you could possibly find on the front of your computer. For example, your console may also have an Infrared port for communicating with a laptop or handheld computer. Even so, become familiar with those few items mentioned in the list. Many computer manuals and software instructions assume that you know where everything is and what it's called.

## What You See: Console — the Back

When it comes to the computer console, the back is definitely more important than the front, and also far uglier. That's where most of the computer's components connect to the console. But other things are worth noting as well:

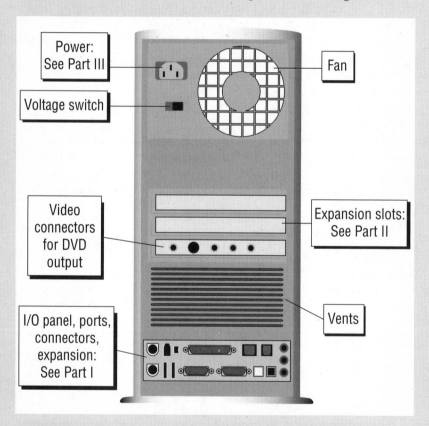

Power: See Part III

Voltage switch

Fan

Video connectors for DVD output

Expansion slots: See Part II

I/O panel, ports, connectors, expansion: See Part I

Vents

- ✔ **Power connector:** The power cord that plugs into the wall gazinta here.

- ✔ **Fan:** Air gets sucked into here, to keep the insides of the console cool.

- ✔ **Voltage switch:** Some power supplies have two operating frequencies. This switch needs to be set only once to match the proper voltage for your country.

- ✔ **Expansion slots:** These are where add-on components and options are installed inside the console. You cannot see them directly, though the slot covers are visible on the back of the console, as shown nearby.

- ✔ **Expansion cards:** These items plug into the expansion slots and reveal a part of themselves on the console's rump, such as the DVD expansion card shown in the illustration.

- ✔ **Vents:** That breathing thing again.

- ✔ **I/O Panel:** Modern PCs put all their connectors in one central location, called the I/O panel. It contains holes for plugging in a variety of goodies. See also Part I to find out what the holes are called and what plugs into them.

The I/O panel may be in one location, as shown in the illustration, or it may be split up into separate areas. For example, you may have one location for the mouse and keyboard connectors, plus another location for other items that attach to the console.

Note that the video connector (for the monitor) is found on either the I/O panel or an expansion card. If it's found in both places, use the connector on the expansion card.

## What You See: Console — the I/O Panel

*I/O* is computer-talk for input and output. The computer's world is all about input and output, and because the console is the center of your computer's world, it plays a major role in that input/output thing. Primarily, the other devices that communicate with the console, to provide it with input or offer it a spot for output, connect to the console, on the console's rear, in a location referred to as the *I/O panel*.

Here are few of the items you can find on the I/O panel:

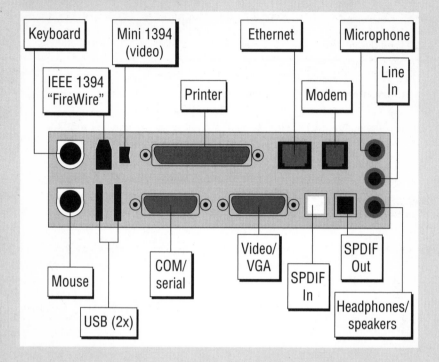

✔ **Keyboard connector:** Where the keyboard plugs into the console. USB keyboards can plug into the USB port as well.

✔ **Mouse connector:** Where the mouse plugs into the console, though USB mice can plug directly into the USB port.

✔ **USB port:** The ever-versatile USB port for the multitude of USB devices to connect to your computer. See also Part II.

✔ **COM (or serial) port:** This once highly versatile connector is now used primarily for external modems and some computer mice. Some consoles may have two COM ports, labeled COM1 and COM2. In the olden days, it was called the RS-232C port. This port's connector has nine pins.

✔ **Video connector:** This is where the monitor connects to the console. It's the same size as the COM port, but sports up to 15 holes. Note that a secondary video connector may be on the back of an expansion card. If so, use that one instead.

✔ **S-Video out:** This connector is used for video output, primarily on PCs with DVD drives or high-end video. You would use the S-View out port to connect the PC to a TV set. (This port isn't shown in the illustration.)

✔ **SPDIF In/Out:** These ports are used to connect the console to high-end audio devices, such as an external sound processor or a stereo system. The connectors use fiber optics to carry the sound signal, which is less susceptible to outside noise than traditional wire connectors. SPDIF stands for Sony/Philips Digital Interconnect Format.

✔ **Microphone jack:** You can plug an optional microphone into this jack for recording your voice or using voice control software.

✔ **Line In jack:** This audio input is used for connecting the PC's sound system to your stereo or VCR, for capturing audio and other sounds.

✔ **Headphones/speaker jack:** This is where you plug in a set of head-phones, to listen privately to your computer, or plug in a set of speakers, for more public listening.

✔ **Modem:** This hole is where you plug a standard phone cord, to connect your computer to the phone jack in the wall. That way, the computer's internal modem can use the telephone to contact the Internet. Modem holes can also be found on expansion cards in some PCs.

✔ **Phone:** This hole is usually found next to the modem jack. It's where you can connect a standard telephone so that you can use a real phone on the same line as the computer. This jack isn't available on every console. Consider it a bonus.

✔ **Ethernet:** This is where the computer connects to a network, or where you connect the computer to a cable or DSL modem. (Networking and the Internet are very similar things.) This hole for this port, also known as an RJ-45, may also appear on the back of an expansion card. See also Part IX.

✔ **Printer port:** The printer plugs in here. This port is also called an LPT, or Centronics, port. That's for the old-timers.

✔ **IEEE 1394 ports:** These ports are similar to USB ports in that they accept a variety of high-speed add-ons, such as external disk drives, scanners, and videocameras. The smaller of the IEEE 1394 ports, called a 1394 "mini," is used primarily to connect digital video. These ports may also be known as *FireWire*.

✔ **Joystick port:** This port can be found on some older PCs, used primarily to connect the old-style joysticks or MIDI musical devices. Today, most of those gizmos are connected by using USB ports.

For more information on plugging stuff in, see also Part I.

# I/O Symbol Table

Connectors, connectors everywhere! They can look similar, or they can be confusing as all get-out. Fortunately, the computer industry understands how confusing connectors can be. To make things easier, many connectors on a PC console not only have unique shapes, but are color coded and often flagged with a specific icon, as shown in the handy nearby table.

Note that the colors aren't an established standard, so some PCs may sport a different color scheme than what's indicated. Also, not every connector is color coded.

Also note that different icons or symbols may be used on different PCs.

| Connector | Symbol | Name | Color |
|---|---|---|---|
| | IOIOI | COM/Serial | Cyan |
| | | Digital video | White |
| | | Ethernet/RJ-45 | None |
| | | IEEE 1394 | None |
| | | IEEE 1394 mini | None |
| | | Infrared | None |
| | | Joystick | Mustard |
| | | Keyboard | Purple |
| | | Line In (audio) | Grey |

| Connector | Symbol | Name | Color |
|---|---|---|---|
| | | Microphone | Pink |
| | | Modem | None |
| | | Monitor | Blue |
| | | Mouse | Green |
| | | Power | Yellow |
| | | Printer | Violet |
| | IN | SPDIF In | Pink/white |
| | OUT | SPDIF Out | Black |
| | | Speakers/Headphones | Lime |
| | | S-Video | Yellow |
| | | USB | None |

# The Basics: What Is a PC?

PC is an acronym for *Personal Computer*, so any type of personal computer, from a handheld or palm computer to a laptop to a desktop and, yes, even the Apple Macintosh, is a personal computer. As long as one person is using the computer, it's a *personal* computer, or PC.

Specifically, the type of computer now labeled a PC is the direct ancestor of the original IBM PC, introduced back in the early 1980s. Though there were other personal computers at that time, they were referred to as *microcomputers* and were used mostly by computer enthusiasts and home hobbyists.

When IBM introduced its own microcomputer, it legitimized the microcomputer and made it "safe" for use in a business environment. Because of the IBM PC's tremendous popularity, it became the standard for all microcomputers. Eventually, any computer that was *compatible* with the original IBM PC (the computer could use the same hardware and run the same software) also was dubbed a PC.

The PC is now the standard computer platform around the world, so much so that being PC or IBM compatible is no longer an issue. Unless the computer says Macintosh or Sun on its case, it's a PC.

Internally, the computer is really nothing more than a very fast, expensive calculator with a larger display and far more buttons. The computer system is composed of two main parts: hardware and software.

## Hardware

*Hardware* is the physical part of the computer. If you can touch it, it's hardware.

The main piece of hardware is the computer's microprocessor, also called the central *p*rocessing *u*nit, or CPU. All other hardware inside the computer (the *console*) is designed to support and serve the microprocessor.

The current type of microprocessor used in the typical PC is the Pentium. There are other variations of this chip as well, given other names depending on the manufacturers and the chips' ability, but Pentium is the big name.

Supporting the Pentium is more hardware. For storage, there's computer memory, or RAM, as well as disk drives. There's also a chipset, which consists of various support hardware that helps control the computer's monitor, networking, power management, and other hardware. All this stuff exists inside the console and lives on a large sheet of green fiberglass called the *motherboard*.

## Software

Hardware by itself is dumb. That's because computer hardware must be controlled by software. Contrary to popular myth, the computer's microprocessor (hardware) isn't the computer's "brain." The computer's brain (if any) is the software that controls and runs the hardware.

The main piece of software in a computer is its *operating system.* That's the main control program. For most PCs, the operating system is Windows, produced by Microsoft Corporation. Other operating systems can also be used on a PC, such as Linux and others, but Windows is by far the most popular PC operating system.

Other software comes in the form of applications or programs that carry out specific tasks. By using various programs, you can direct the computer to perform a variety of services. Indeed, it's this versatility that has kept the PC popular and useful over the past 25 years or so.

- ✓ Computer software is nothing more than instructions that tell the hardware what to do, how to act, or when to lose your data.

- ✓ Although computer software comes on disks (CDs or floppy disks), the *disks* aren't software. Software is stored on disks just as music is stored on cassettes and CDs.

- ✓ You never have to learn about programming to use a computer. Someone else does the programming; then, you buy the program (the software) to get your work done.

## You

That last part of your computer system is you, the computer operator. Though software controls the hardware, it's you who controls the software, by telling it what you want done.

The computer does whatever you want it to do. Its flexibility and potential is really unlimited. If you want a system to help you compose music, you can assemble the proper hardware and software to make that happen. If you want to run a business, that can be done too. The flexibility and configuration possibilities of the PC are endless, which is why the PC has remained the best-selling, most useful computer platform in the universe.

# The Basics: Types and Models of PCs

There's no such thing as the *typical* PC. Not only does each manufacturer add its own touches of design and style, but different and various configurations are available. They're all PCs, but how they look and — most importantly — how they sit on your desk divides them into various subclasses. Here's the rundown:

- ✔ **Desktop:** The original IBM PC sat flat and square on top of a desk, which is why that and similar modes are referred to as desktop computers. Typically, the monitor is set right on top of the slablike console.

- ✔ **Desktop (small footprint):** This is basically the same arrangement as the traditional desktop, though the console is considerably smaller — often, too small to set the monitor atop the console. The footprint refers to how much desk space the console occupies.

- ✔ **Minitower:** This is the most popular PC configuration, which is essentially a small-footprint desktop on its side, though the PC isn't really sideways. The console is small enough to sit on top of your desk, with the monitor sitting right next to it.

- ✔ **Notebook or laptop:** This is a portable version of the PC, usually the size of a typical three-ring binder or coffee-table book. Yes, they manage to squeeze everything in a desktop PC into a portable, battery-powered, convenient unit. Despite their heftier price tags, laptops are very popular and often outsell desktop PCs.

- ✔ **Towers:** An older style of PC that can still be found is the tower unit, which is like the minitower, but considerably taller and with more room inside the console. These boxes are mostly found in the "back office" of businesses, where they control the network or are used to prop up one end of a wobbly table.

# The Basics: Inside the Console

You find nestled inside the console the core elements of a computer. These are the basic elements of the computer system, the electronic orchestra through which the PC plays its tune. The location of these gizmos varies from computer to computer, but, if you're curious, the following list details some of the more important elements:

- ✔ **Power supply:** This item serves two purposes. First, it converts the AC current from the wall into DC current to drive the motherboard and devices inside the console. Second, the power supply houses the fan that keeps the console's insides cool. The power supply connects to each internal disk drive as well as to the motherboard. It also connects to the power button.

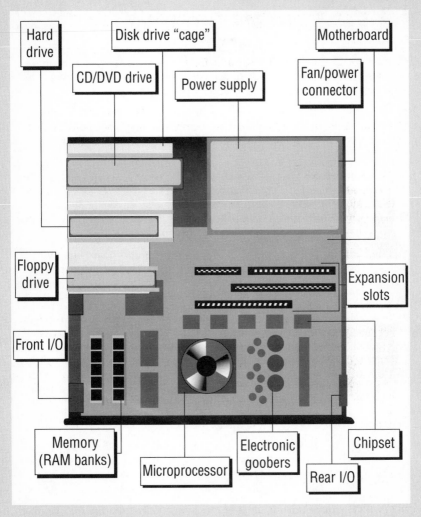

- **Hard drive**
- **Disk drive "cage"**
- **Motherboard**
- **CD/DVD drive**
- **Power supply**
- **Fan/power connector**
- **Floppy drive**
- **Expansion slots**
- **Front I/O**
- **Memory (RAM banks)**
- **Microprocessor**
- **Electronic goobers**
- **Chipset**
- **Rear I/O**

- ✔ **Motherboard:** This is the main circuitry board inside the console, the home base for the PC's microprocessor, memory, chipset, and other vital components.

- ✔ **Disk drive cage:** This metal structure is used to hold the various disk drives installed in the console as well as provide space for more disk drives.

- ✔ **CD-ROM/DVD drive:** The drive is installed in the disk drive cage, but in one of the places where the drive can be accessed from outside the console (so that you can insert and remove CDs or DVDs). The drive also connects to the power supply and to a special connector on the motherboard.

*BP-15*

✔ **Hard drive:** This drive lives inside the console's drive cage, but doesn't need to have access to outside the case. The hard drive is connected to the power supply and the motherboard.

✔ **Floppy drive:** Like the CD-ROM/DVD drive, this drive is installed in the console's drive cage with outside access. The floppy drive is connected to the power supply and the motherboard.

✔ **Memory:** The computer's memory, or RAM, is installed into a series of banks on the motherboard. Memory comes in tiny expansion card modules, called DIMMs. These plug into corresponding slots on the motherboard.

✔ **Microprocessor:** This is the main chip. The boss. The CPU. All the other electronics inside the console are designed to work well with and serve the microprocessor. Today's PCs come with high-speed, high-power microprocessors that require extra cooling; the microprocessor wears a special little fan like a hat, which helps keep it cool.

✔ **Chipset:** One or more computer chips on the motherboard supply the computer's basic personality (so to speak). These chips control input/output (I/O) as well as the basic configuration of the computer's monitor, keyboard, mouse, networking, and other main components.

✔ **Expansion slots:** Designed for internal expansion of the computer, expansion slots aren't as plentiful as in years past. This is because most of the features previously added via *expansion cards* (networking, modem, more memory) are now part of the chipset on the motherboard. Even so, expansion slots remain inside the console and allow you to further add to or configure your PC. Expansion cards plug into expansion slots, like adding new shelves inside a cupboard.

There are three types of expansion slots:

- **ISA:** The traditional type of expansion slot of ancient design (available on the first IBM PC, 25 years ago), and still used today for many simple hardware add-ons. ISA stands for Industry Standard Architecture. A typical PC has at least one of these slots available.

- **PCI:** A more advanced type of expansion slot than ISA. PCI stands for Peripheral Component Interconnect. Most PCs have at least one of these slots, if not more. (It depends on the size of the console.)

- **AGP:** An expansion slot designed specifically for advanced, high-end graphics cards. AGP stands for Accelerated Graphics Port. Not every motherboard has this slot. (Lesser graphics adapters plug into a PCI slot or are included in the chipset.)

✔ **I/O:** The motherboard's reach extends beyond the console's physical space, thanks to a host of I/O ports and connectors, located on the back and often the front of the console. These connectors are plugged into the motherboard via special cables.

There are many more technical details about your console's innards and the motherboard specifically, most of which aren't really necessary to know for the casual computer operator.

Be aware of your computer's microprocessor and its name and horsepower. Often, this information is displayed when the computer first starts — though you have to be quick to catch it.

It also helps to know the quantity of RAM installed in the console. Computers crave RAM, especially when they're running high-end graphics programs or complex computer games.

The expansion slots provide a way to add more internal components to your PC, though for starting out, the motherboard contains just about everything you need. Still, be aware that it's possible to add more features and abilities by simply purchasing and installing a new expansion card. See also "The Basics: Adding Hardware."

It isn't necessary to open your PC. Please do not do so unless directed to by tech support or when you're installing or upgrading your computer. When doing so, be sure to turn off *and* unplug the console before opening it up and looking inside.

# The Basics: Adding Hardware

The beauty of the computer is that it can be endlessly expanded or upgraded. The computer you own today probably won't look the same a month or a year down the road. It's the PC's ability to be expanded and improved on that has made it one of the most successful computer hardware designs ever.

There are two ways to add new hardware to your computer system: internally or externally.

## Internal expansion

Internal hardware is added to the PC by plugging an expansion card into one of the expansion slots on the console's motherboard. At one time, this was about the only way you could add more memory, better video, networking, or a special modem. Today, however, most of that stuff is included with the chipset on the motherboard. Even so, expansion slots remain for many purposes, which allows you to customize your PC any way you want.

Popular expansion cards let you add video support for a second monitor, a more advanced video adapter, a secondary network adapter, a satellite modem card, custom sound cards, cards to support more disk drives, cards to add more ports (USB/IEEE) — the variety is almost endless.

Beyond expansion cards, your console may have extra room for more memory or disk drives inside its drive cage. It may even be possible to replace the microprocessor with a better, faster version (though such an upgrade is often financially impractical).

Before going nuts, however, ensure that your PC has ample internal expansion options. The drive cage must have room for an extra hard drive, for example. And, you need to ensure that you have open expansion slots — and slots of the right type — for whatever expansion card options you crave.

If expansion is your goal, get a minitower or full-size tower PC. Those models often come with more expansion slots and drive cage "bays" than the smaller-format PCs.

## External expansion

Everything that plugs into the console can be considered external expansion, though certain key parts of the PC aren't really expansion "options." The keyboard, mouse, and monitor are necessary to the PC's basic operations. Even the printer and modem can arguably be considered basic PC components and not expansion options.

Generally speaking, true expansion options plug into the PC via one of the ports — usually, the USB port. The IEEE port is also popular. Once upon a time, the COM, or serial, port was popular as well, but these days external expansion of your PC system is most likely done by adding a device, or a number of devices, to the USB or IEEE ports.

The most popular external expansion options are as follows:

- **Scanners:** The scanner lets you create a graphical image for the computer by using anything that's flat. You can scan old photographs or your kid's artwork or even use the scanner with special software to read text.

- **Digital cameras:** You can connect a digital camera to your computer for copying, or *downloading,* images. After they're in the computer, you can photo-edit those images, e-mail them, create a slideshow, print them, or do a number of miraculous things.

- **Videocameras:** You can connect a videocamera to your PC directly for use in online chats or for online meetings, by creating your own *webcam.* You can also connect a videocamera to transfer your home movies. Special software can be used to edit those movies and create your own DVDs.

✔ **External hard drives:** This is possibly the most popular external expansion item to add to a PC, because adding the extra storage doesn't involve opening the console's case. By using the USB or IEEE port, you can add one or several external hard drives to your PC, to make more storage available for your videos, music, photographs, or anything you create with your PC.

✔ **External CD and DVD drives:** Another popular item to add is another CD or DVD drive, especially one that can record CDs or DVDs. Adding these drives externally is much easier than adding one internally, especially for the beginner.

Numerous other expansion options exist. In fact, the list is long enough that it would make quite a thick book by itself. For the variety, simply check a computer catalog, online store, or retail computer store near you. See also Part I for information on connecting things to the console.

# The Basics: Windows

The computer's operating system, Windows, is in charge of the entire computer. It does things you would never imagine, menial tasks and duties that are obscure yet necessary. Fortunately, Windows has been honed over the years, and, despite the complexity of the PC, with Windows in charge, your duties as a computer operator aren't really that complex or involved.

Basically, Windows has four duties:

✔ **Present an interface for you, the human, to use the computer.** This interface is the *desktop,* used to display information and graphically represent things inside the computer.

✔ **Manage the computer's hardware.** This is pretty much an automatic chore, though Windows lets you manipulate certain hardware settings, such as the monitor's resolution or whether your stuff is printed longways or tallways on the printer. But most of the mundane things — keeping the time, fetching information from disk, performing minor maintenance — are done in the background automatically.

✔ **Manage software.** The applications you install rely on Windows as a bridge between what they do and the hardware inside the PC that makes all that stuff possible. Windows also prevents programs from running amok and, when they do, keeps them contained as best it can so that the system doesn't come crashing down.

✔ **Manage the files and stuff you create.** Windows helps you store information on your computer so that you can find it again later when you need it. It helps you keep track of things and provides tools to help you organize and order all your stuff.

Most of the time you use Windows, you work in your applications programs and process words, work a database, send e-mail, and do other typical computer tasks. You use Windows occasionally to set up or reconfigure your computer's hardware, add new software, or work with the files you create. Beyond that, Windows is simply the program in charge. See also Part IV, which tells you where important things are located in Windows.

## The Basics: The Internet

Once upon a time, the Internet was considered a minor part of the PC's existence. Today, PCs and the Internet walk hand-in-hand. Using the Internet, particularly e-mail, is the number-one reason that most people buy a new PC. Because of this, all new PCs come equipped with all the hardware you need to access the Internet. All the software (or most of the important programs) also comes with the operating system, Windows.

The Internet itself isn't a computer. The Internet is not a program or any software you can own. Instead, the Internet is hundreds of thousands of computers all over the world. They're connected together and they share, store, and swap information.

You can use your PC to access the Internet, where your computer joins the thousands of others already on the Internet. After it's connected, you use various software programs to access information on the Internet. These are the most common programs or things accessed on the Internet:

✔ **The World Wide Web:** This is a convenient way to view information stored on computers all over the world. The Web displays information the same as you would read text in a newspaper or magazine: very friendly with pictures. The various Web *pages* also contain links to other, related information or similar Web pages. Visiting those pages is as easy as clicking the links.

✔ **E-mail:** Everyone using the Internet can send or receive messages by using electronic mail, or *e-mail*. Accounts are available all over, and many at no charge. By using e-mail, you can send messages to other Internet users as well as send files, photos, music, videos, and just about any type of information imaginable.

✔ **File transfer:** The Internet is a vast library of stored files and information. You can access those files by transferring them from the Internet into your computer. Some of the files are free programs you can use to further expand the abilities of your PC.

You use a modem — either a dial-up modem or a high-speed cable, DSL, or satellite modem — to gain access to the Internet. You can also get on the Internet through a local-area network, as long as the network is connected to the Internet. (This is how you get on the Internet at large companies or at school.)

For most individuals and home users, you need to sign up for Internet service with an *ISP*. These are local or national companies whose purpose is to connect folks to the Internet — like a cable company offers you cable TV. (In fact, most cable TV companies also offer Internet access.) ISPs are listed in the Yellow Pages.

The only other thing you need to access the Internet is money; ISPs, like the cable company, require a monthly fee. (It's possible to use the Internet for free at a public library, but that's not this book's subject.)

# The Basics: Your Stuff

Having a PC is about Windows, the Internet, and software, but all that really boils down to you and the stuff you create or collect. That information is stored on the computer in the form of *files*.

A file can contain any type of information. For example, a file can be a simple text document. It can be a list of folks you want to invite to a party. A file can also be a graphical image, a song, a movie. Programs are files. This chapter is a file on my computer. Files are chunks of information stored in a computer.

Files are created in the computer's memory. (They can also be retrieved from the Internet or copied from other computers, but even then the files originated in some computer's memory bank somewhere.) From memory, files are saved on a computer's hard drive, which is the most reliable location for the safe, long-term storage of computer information.

Windows helps you keep track of your files in several ways. First, you give a file a name when it's saved to disk. Windows also gives the file an *icon,* or tiny picture, that helps you associate the type of file you created. Special icons exist for documents, music files, videos, and other types.

A Folder    Text Document.txt    Sound file.wav    Graphics file.bmp

Program.exe    video file.wmv    web page.htm    unknown file

The date and time the file was saved to disk are also included with the file information, along with how much disk space the file occupies. Windows keeps all this information, but you can use it as well.

Windows helps you keep your files organized by using *folders*. Folders contain files, so files relating to the same project or files of a similar type can be kept together. And, the folders can contain even more folders, so you can be seriously organized if that's your goal. See also Part VII.

# Part I

# Connecting Stuff

**I**f your life's technical experience includes only plugging something into the wall, boy, are you in for a surprise!

Yes, computers do plug into the wall — several times and in several ways. More than that, computer gadgets and gizmos plug into each other. Unlike your stereo system, where most of the cables look alike, on the computer just about every cable is different: different shape, different color, different way to plug it in. This chapter covers the basics of plugging stuff in.

## In this part . . .

## *About Computer Cables*

A computer cable is described by which port it plugs into and its length.

For example, to connect a printer to the console, you use a printer cable. A USB device (including printers) connects by using a USB cable. A monitor uses a monitor cable.

One exception is networking, which is done by using Cat-5 cable, though you can say "networking cable" and the guy in the computer store won't mock you. The connector on the console is called an RJ-45, but networking cable isn't "RJ-45 cable." It's Cat-5.

Some cables are permanently attached to their devices: The mouse and keyboard have such cables, for example. Other cables are separate. That just means that you must remember to plug in both ends.

Cable length is measured in feet or meters. USB, IEEE, networking, printer, and serial cables all come in varying lengths.

Good news: Nearly all computer cables are what they call *idiot-proof.* That means you can plug them in only one way. You cannot plug in a computer cable backward or incorrectly or in any manner that may damage your computer or the device being plugged in.

But, unless the hardware documentation says so otherwise, it's okay to plug in most computer gizmos while the computer is on. There are some exceptions to this rule, so carefully read through the other sections in this part of the book!

Some computer devices plug right into the wall. Some don't plug into the wall at all. And some devices use what's called a *power brick,* or *transformer,* which is either part of the plug itself or living on the cable between the device and the wall socket.

## *Audio*

PCs have built-in sound, and the console has a teensy, crappy speaker. What you really need are external speakers. Plus, you can use a microphone or headphones or attach an audio cable to any sound-producing device and record that sound on your PC. This is all done thanks to the PC's audio connectors.

All PC audio connectors are of the *mini-DIN* design. That's a common connector-hole combination used on many audio devices. If your audio device doesn't use mini-DIN (for example, standard headphones, which use a much larger connector), you can buy an adapter at any electronics or music store.

- ✏ PC speakers connect to the Line Out, speaker, or headphone jack on the console.

- ✏ Microphones connect to the microphone connector.

- ✏ The Line In connector is used to connect any nonamplified sound source, such as your stereo, VCR, phonograph, Victrola, or other sound-generating device.

Yes, the difference between the Line In and microphone jack is that Line In devices aren't amplified.

Your console may have multiple sets of audio connectors: three on the front, three on the back, three on the DVD adapter card. If so, use the sound connectors on the DVD card first because they're the best. Otherwise, when audio connectors are on the front and back of the PC, the front set is simply a copy or spare (designed for easy hookup of the mic or headphones).

To record sound, you need software that lets you convert audio input into digital storage inside the computer.

## Digital Camera

Your digital camera may connect to the console in one of three ways:

- ✏ Through the USB port

- ✏ Through the mini-IEEE port

- ✏ Through its own, special cable

The connection used by your camera depends on the camera's manufacturer, not on the PC.

Note that it's also possible to use a media card reader on your PC to directly read the camera's digital "film." For example, you can get a CompactFlash memory reader, which you connect to your PC by using the USB port (see also "USB Port").

See also "Optical Audio," for information on using that specialized connector.

## IEEE

The IEEE port allows you to use high-speed external devices with your PC. This port isn't as common as the USB port, though the IEEE port behaves in much the same way, and for some devices (external disk drives, digital video, high-end scanners), it's better than USB.

IEEE devices require an IEEE cable, which may or may not come with the device.

The cable's ends are identical. It matters not which end of the cable goes into the device or which end plugs into the console.

As with USB, it's possible to *daisy-chain* IEEE devices, by plugging one into another, into another, and finally into the console. Note that certain IEEE gadgets prefer to be connected to the console directly.

Also like USB is the IEEE hub, which allows you to expand the number of IEEE ports.

Some devices, particularly digital videocameras, use the mini-IEEE connector. This connector requires a unique cable. (It uses only four wires, whereas the standard IEEE cable has six.)

 IEEE is also known as 1394. The two names are often used together, as in IEEE 1394. On Apple computers, the IEEE interface is referred to as *FireWire*. No matter what the name, the standard symbol is shown in the margin.

Most PCs don't come with IEEE ports, though they can be added easily by installing inexpensive expansion cards.

# Joystick

An older PC may sport a unique joystick port. It's a 25-pin, D-shell connector, found on the rumps of older-model computers. The joystick port can also be used to connect the MIDI adapter for playing musical instruments with your PC.

Today's joysticks plug into the USB port (see also "USB Port").

The joystick port may also be referred to as the A/D port, where A/D stands for *a*nalog-to-*d*igital.

# Keyboard

The PC keyboard plugs into the keyboard port on the back of the console.

Note that the keyboard port looks amazingly similar to the mouse port. Despite their visual similarity, they're two different ports. Your keyboard (or mouse) doesn't work when it's plugged into the wrong port.

A USB keyboard can plug into any USB port.

Some USB keyboards come with lime green adapters, designed to convert the USB ports into keyboard port connectors. Using this type of adapter is optional.

Don't plug the keyboard into the keyboard port while the computer is on. It's okay to plug in a USB keyboard, but don't plug anything into the keyboard port when the computer is on. It may damage the keyboard, the computer, or both.

# Microphone

To use a microphone with your PC, plug it into the microphone port. See also "Audio."

# Modem

Most PCs are sold with internal modems. In that case, all you see on the back of the console is a standard phone jack. Take a phone cord, plug it into the modem's phone jack, and then plug the other end of the phone cord into the telephone company's jack on the wall. The modem is connected.

If the modem has a second phone jack, one designed for a telephone, you can plug a telephone's cord into that jack as well. You can use the phone any time the computer isn't using the modem to make a call.

External modems also have phone jacks and need to be plugged in the same way as internal modems. Additionally, the external modem needs to plug into the console. This is done by either using a serial cable and plugging the modem into the console's COM port or using a USB cable. External modems must also be plugged into the wall for power.

Don't plug the modem into the network's RJ-45 jack. Although that hole looks the same, it's slightly larger and the phone jack doesn't stay put.

# Monitor

The monitor plugs into the VGA, or graphics adapter, jack on the back of the console. It goes in only one way.

If the console has two VGA connectors, you probably want to use the one on an expansion card rather than the one on the console's I/O panel. (See also the "Big Picture.")

# Mouse

Your computer's mouse plugs into the mouse port on the back of the console. This port looks exactly like the keyboard port, but be sure that you plug the mouse into the right port. The mouse doesn't work otherwise.

USB mice need to connect to the USB port, though many mouse manufacturers also include an adapter that lets you convert the USB connector to a PC mouse port connector. Either way works.

Turn your computer off before you connect or disconnect the mouse to the mouse port.

# Network

To connect your PC to a network, or to a networklike device, such as a cable or DSL modem, plug the cable's plastic connector into the console's RJ-45 jack.

The RJ-45 jack looks exactly like a telephone connector, though it's more squat (wider and shorter).

When the network cable is fully inserted, you feel or hear it snap into place.

To remove the network cable, press the tab on the narrow end, and then slide the cable out of the hole — just like you disconnect a phone cord.

# Optical Audio

If you're a high-end audio snob, you can use optical audio to connect the PC to your high-end optical audio sound equipment. Both devices, input and output, must have optical audio. And, you must obtain special (and not cheap) fiber-optic cable to connect the toys.

Optical audio isn't a must.

Be careful not to bang, touch, or taunt the clear glass ends of the optical cable. Better cables come with little protective caps that you can keep on the ends when the cable isn't connected.

Optical Audio Out ports connect to optical Audio In, and vice versa.

# Power

Cinchy: The plug goes into the wall socket.

Some power cables are affixed to the device they power. Others must be plugged in at both ends. Oftentimes, it's that second end disconnecting that's the source of endless computer angst and woe.

You may want to use a power strip or UPS. See also Part III for information on turning on your PC.

# Printer

The printer plugs into the console's printer port. Nothing could be more "duh."

The standard PC printer cable has two different ends. One is designed to plug into the printer; the other, into the console. It's impossible to confuse the two.

USB printers plug in by using a USB cable. For printers with both printer and USB options, use the USB option.

Printers don't come with cables! You must buy the cable — USB or standard printer cable — separately.

Another name for the printer port is LPT1. Another name for the printer cable is *Centronics. Another* name for the port is *parallel port,* with the corresponding *parallel cable.*

Avoid inexpensive printer cables because they aren't bidirectional. You should ensure that you get a printer cable that talks both ways. That way, you can use all your printer's features.

It's trivial, but printer cables should be no more than about 10 feet long. The signal may degrade over longer distances. Well, and you get tired of walking over to a printer set far away.

Printers can also be connected to computers over the network, in which case the printer is connected by using a networking cable only.

# S-Video

S-Video connectors allow you to send your computer's video output to a standard television set, or to any video gizmo that has S-Video input.

S-Video output provides higher-quality images than other types of video output. You typically find this type of connector only on the rumps of PCs with high-end video adapters.

S-Video is typically output only. To read video input on your PC, you need a special video adapter that accepts input.

The final thing to remember about S-Video is that it's video only; it doesn't transmit any audio. To get the sound over to your television, you have to string some wires from the Line Out, speaker, or headphone jacks or use the optical audio connections (if your television supports that).

# Scanner

Most scanners connect to the console by using the USB port. In fact, they don't even require a power cable; the scanner draws its power from the USB port itself. Amazing.

High-end scanners use the IEEE port rather than, or in addition to, USB.

# Serial

Today, the most common device to plug into the console's serial, or COM, port is an external dial-up modem. There are also serial mice as well as a few serial printers.

At one time, a serial port was the most versatile type of connector on your PC. Today, however, it's kept around mostly for compatibility with older devices.

On consoles with more than one serial port, they're named COM1, COM2, and so on.

COM is short for *comm*unications.

Another term for the serial port is RS-232.

# Speakers

Speakers plug into the speaker or headphone jack (see also "Audio").

Note that speakers can also be a part of the monitor. Even so, a separate cable is required in order to plug the speakers into the speaker or headphone jack on the console.

# USB Port

USB devices plug into the USB port — any USB port, though some devices specifically want to be connected to the console or to a powered USB port.

Newer USB devices are generally faster and better than the original USB standard. These newer devices are referred to as high-speed or USB 2.0 devices, and they require a USB 2.0 port. Most PCs come with this port, though older PCs can add the port by adding an internal expansion card.

USB cables have two different ends, dubbed A and B. The A end is flat and exists on the console or the back of any USB hub. The B end is trapezoidal in shape and plugs into the USB device.

USB extension cables are available, but be sure that the extension cable's ends match what you're plugging into: A to A or B to B.

USB hubs allow you to further expand the number of USB devices your computer can use. The hub connects to the console (or to another hub) by using a standard A-B USB cable. The hub itself contains more USB ports, from two to four, on up to a dozen or more.

Some hubs must be plugged in to help supply external USB devices with power. These are known as *powered hubs.*

Many USB devices act as hubs and provide even more USB connectors for even more gizmos.

USB cables come in a variety of lengths, but the cables are never longer than 3 or 4 feet. Any longer and the signal may be compromised.

USB devices can be connected or disconnected whether the power is on or off. If the power is on, the computer instantly recognizes the device and makes it available. But note that some USB devices, particularly external disk drives and other storage devices, cannot be removed unless you first use the PC's operating system to disconnect, or *unmount,* the device.

# Wireless Gizmos

Yes, even wireless devices require some type of wired connection.

For example, a wireless keyboard and mouse require you to connect the transmitter to the keyboard and mouse ports or to a USB connector on the console. Beyond that point, however, the keyboard and mouse aren't tethered to the console by wires.

Wireless networking is generally wire-free. The network card's antenna sticks out of the console's rump. (On a laptop, the antenna may be internal.) Despite the term *wireless,* at some point the system uses wires. For example, a wireless hub needs to connect to the Internet, and that's done by using a wire.

# Part II

# Installing Hardware and Software

Believe it or not, you are the master of your PC's domain. You control what goes into the computer system, whether it's hardware or software. You get to not only choose which hardware or software to add, but also install it all by yourself. This isn't as crazy as fixing your toaster or as delicate as brain surgery. In fact, it's deceptively easy — but don't tell that to the overpriced computer consultants and fix-it shops!

## In this part . . .

# *The Add Hardware Icon*

The Control Panel's Add Hardware icon seems like it should be used to help add new hardware to your computer. That's only half true. You need to use the Add Hardware icon only when the computer poops out and fails to recognize newly installed hardware. As PCs become more sophisticated, those instances are fewer.

To access the Add Hardware icon, heed these steps:

*1.* Click the Start button to display its menu.

*2.* Choose Control Panel from the menu.

*3.* If Category view is being used, click the text labeled Switch to Classic View.

Classic view displays all the Control Panels' icons, which may be confusing, but it's more useful than Category view. This figure shows an example of Classic view.

 *4.* Double-click the Add Hardware icon.

Opening the Add Hardware icon runs the Add Hardware Wizard.

*5.* Read the wizard's instructions and click the Next button to continue.

*6.* Work through the wizard.

Heed the instructions that are offered, and make selections and click the Next button as required.

7. Click the Finish button when you're done.

See also "Adding New Hardware."

# The Add or Remove Programs Icon

Most software comes with its own install or uninstall programs. When those don't work, or they aren't obvious, you can use the Windows Control Panel and its Add or Remove Programs icon for your software installation and removal chores.

Here's how to access the Add or Remove Programs icon:

1. Open a Windows Explorer window; from the desktop, open the My Computer icon.

   Or, you can press Win+E.

2. From the Address bar drop-down list, choose Control Panel.

3. Ensure that Classic view is chosen.

   Refer to the preceding section.

 4. Open the Add or Remove Programs icon.

   Opening the icon displays the Add or Remove Programs window, which can be used in several ways, depending on which of the buttons on the window's left side are selected.

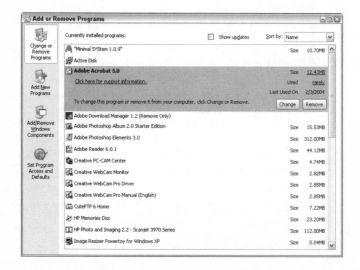

There can be as many as four buttons, depending on your version of Windows XP:

✓ **Change or Remove Programs:** This option lists all installed software in your computer and allows you to select one to remove. Options to change installed programs are also available, depending on the program. See also "Software Installation and Removal" and "Uninstalling software."

✓ **Add New Programs:** This is the item to choose when you need extra help in finding and installing new software.

✓ **Add/Remove Windows Components:** Choose this item to install or remove programs that come with Windows. See also "Adding Windows Components."

✓ **Set Program Access and Defaults:** These advanced options control access to certain programs.

You can close the Add or Remove Programs window when you're done messing around.

## Adding New Hardware

The best way to add new hardware is to follow the instructions offered with the hardware. The instructions tell you what to do, and in what order, and perhaps offer helpful suggestions.

Read through the instructions once before installing or adding the new hardware. Then, read through them a second time as you go through the steps.

Windows instantly recognizes most new PC hardware you shove into or attach behind the console. Read the instructions anyway.

When you plug in new USB or IEEE devices, you may hear the computer beep and see a pop-up message where the PC tells you how excited it is about the new device.

Hardware requires software in order to run. In some cases, the software could just be Windows itself, but, many times, additional software is required in order to power the new hardware, and it must be installed. It's important to follow the software installation instructions properly; sometimes, the new hardware must be installed before the software, and sometimes it works the other way.

Before adding internal components, such as an expansion card or more memory, be sure to turn off *and* unplug the computer's console.

After adding some new hardware devices, it's necessary to restart Windows.

If Windows fails to recognize the new hardware, use the Add Hardware icon in the Control Panel (see also "The Add Hardware Icon"). Note that modems and non-USB joysticks must be installed by using other icons in the Control Panel:

  ✔ To add a new external modem to your PC, use the Phone and Modem Options icon in the Control Panel.

  ✔ To add a non-USB joystick to your PC, use the Game Controllers icon in the Control Panel.

 Adding new hardware may force Windows XP to require reactivation. Microsoft does this to ensure that all the new hardware is compatible with Windows XP, and also to thwart sneaky software pirates. You must contact Microsoft, either by phone or via the Internet, to reactivate your copy of Windows XP. Obey the instructions on the screen, if any.

# Adding Windows Components

Windows comes with a host of optional programs, utilities, and stuff, all of which you can add or remove as you wish. These include programs like Paint, Notepad, WordPad, all those games, and other random software.

Adding more programs gives you more options and things to do in Windows.

Removing programs, especially those you seldom use, frees up disk space.

To add or remove these Windows components, use the Add or Remove Programs icon in the Control Panel. See also "The Add or Remove Programs Icon."

 After the Add or Remove Programs window is open, click the Add/Remove Windows Components button. It runs a wizard that helps you install or remove the various programs that come with Windows.

The wizard displays various categories of programs. To view the contents of a category, select the category and click the Details button. For example, to view the Accessories and Utilities category, click to select it and then click the Details button, as shown in the figure. Then, to view the contents of the Games category, select it and click the Details button.

To add a program, place a check mark by its name.

To remove *(uninstall)* a program, remove its check mark.

Check marks in gray boxes indicate that not every program in that category has been installed.

Keep an eye on the Total Disk Space Required value.

After making your selections, click the Next button. Wait as the options are installed or removed. Click the Finish button when you're done.

In some instances, you need to restart Windows after clicking the Finish button.

## Removing a game

As an example of removing a Windows component, here are the steps you would take to remove the Solitaire game:

*1.* Open the Windows Components Wizard.

*2.* Click to select Accessories and Utilities.

*3.* Click the Details button.

*4.* Click to select Games.

*5.* Click the Details button.

*6.* Click to remove the check mark by Solitaire.

*7.* Click OK once to close the Games window. Click OK again to close the Accessories and Utilities window.

*8.* Click the Next button.

   Windows removes the game.

*9.* Click the Finish button.

You're done.

## Adding Fax Services

As an example of adding a Windows component, the following steps describe how to install the Windows Fax tool. This tool may not be available in all versions of Windows.

*1.* Open the Windows Components Wizard.

*2.* Click to put a check mark by the Fax Services item.

This item is at the main level. Note that for other items you may have to click to select an item and then click the Details button — perhaps twice or more — to get to the specific component you want.

*3.* Click the Next button.

Windows installs the necessary files.

You may be asked to insert the original Windows CD to complete installation. If you don't have this CD, you're stuck.

*4.* Click the Finish button.

You're done.

# Inserting an Expansion Card

Anyone who is good with Legos or Tinker Toys can add an expansion card to a PC. The specific steps for each card vary, and you should follow the directions included with the card. I've listed these steps as a general outline:

*1.* Turn off and unplug the PC's console.

*2.* Open the PC's console.

Use a screwdriver to remove the screws on the back of the console. Note that some consoles don't have screws, and the screws aren't always on the back. Good luck!

*3.* Locate the proper expansion slot.

The expansion card is an ISA, PCI, or AGP card. You must find the corresponding slot on the motherboard for that card.

PCI slot      ISA slot

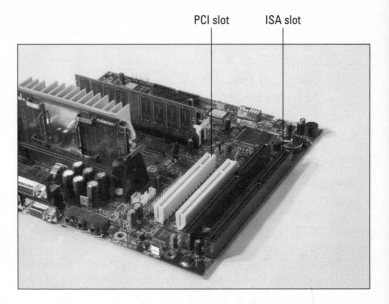

Yes, you may have to move some cables out of the way. This is okay, as long as you don't disconnect any of the cables — or as long as you remember to reconnect any you've disconnected.

Some PCI or ISA slots may not be available because of other items inside the console blocking them. Make sure that you choose a slot that has enough room around it to accommodate your expansion card.

4. Remove the ISA/PCI slot's back cover.

   This small metal cover is just behind the slot. It's where an expansion card's rump is accessible to the world. Remove the slot cover and toss it out — but keep the tiny screw (if a screw is used).

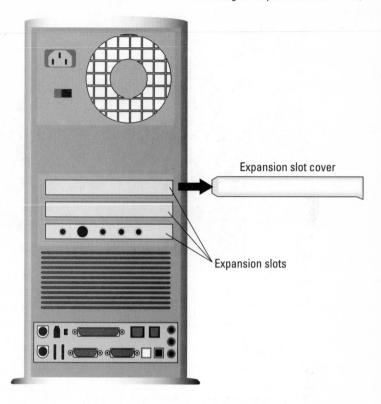

Expansion slot cover

Expansion slots

5. Remove the expansion card from its sealed bag.

   Carefully handle the card! Try to touch it only by the edges. Don't touch the components or any metal part of the card.

   It helps if you can keep one hand on the console's metal case while you're handling the expansion card. This precaution zeroes the electrical potential between you, the case, and the card and reduces the chance of that evil static electricity damaging something.

6. Set any options on the card.

   Some cards have tiny switches that must be set in order to preconfigure the card — though this isn't as common as it once was.

7. Insert the card into the slot.

   Be firm, but gentle. The card can go in only one way. It also has to seat itself on the back of the computer, where you removed the slot's back cover in Step 4.

8. Optionally, connect any cables or wires that the expansion card needs.

9. Screw down the expansion card's back cover.

   Use the screw you took from Step 4. Or, if a clamping or non-screw system is used, do whatever it takes to firmly secure the card.

10. Double-check everything.

    Are all the cables connected? Everything in snug? No loose items rattling about? No screwdriver left on the motherboard? No flashlight lurking inside the case?

11. Close up the console.

12. Reconnect the power cord.

13. Turn on the console and the computer.

Adding an expansion card could trigger the reactivation of Windows XP. See also "Adding New Hardware."

## Installing Memory

Adding more memory to your PC is one great — and inexpensive — way to boost your system's performance. It's simple. Follow these general steps, though if any specific steps come with your computer's memory, be sure to follow them instead:

*1.* Turn off and unplug the PC's console.

*2.* Open the PC's console.

Remove the screws from the back of the console, or use what-ever clever method is required in order to open that sucker up.

*3.* Locate the memory banks.

There should be a collection of them, usually two or four grouped side-by-side.

Memory DIMM

Memory banks (two slots)

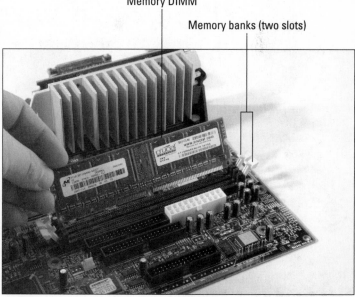

*4.* Remove any old memory, if necessary.

Hopefully you just have to add your new memory cards, or DIMMs, into empty slots. But you may have to remove older memory to make room for the new DIMMs. If so, see the follow-ing section. Then, come back here to finish installation.

*5.* Move aside the connectors on the side of the memory slot.

Two plastic arms swing up to help hold down the DIMM. Swing them out of the way now.

Plastic clips

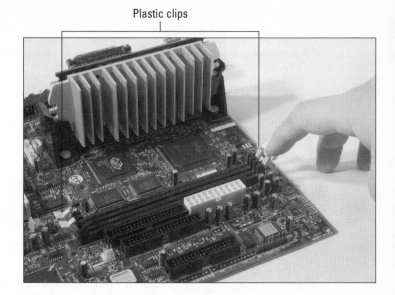

6. **Remove the new memory from its sealed bag or tube.**

   Be careful with those DIMMs! Touch them only by their edges.

   It helps if you use one hand to hold the DIMM and keep the other hand touching the console's metal case. This precaution zeroes the electrical potential between the memory, the case, and yourself. By doing so, you reduce the chance of generating static electricity and damaging the delicate memory chips.

7. **Line up the DIMM with the slot.**

   The DIMM and the slot are keyed so that you can insert the memory only one way. Try to line up the DIMM so that it's properly positioned over the slot.

DIMM

Notches                Clip

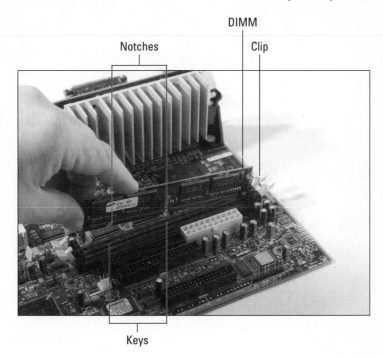

Keys

**8.** Plug the DIMM into the slot.

Firmly, but gently. Do not force! If the thing doesn't seat properly, it's most likely oriented improperly. Turn it around and
try again.

**9.** Double-check everything.

Are all the cables connected? Everything in snug? No loose
items rattling about? No screwdriver left on the motherboard?
No flashlight lurking inside the case? Your fly zipped up?

**10.** Close up the console.

**11.** Reconnect the power cord.

**12.** Turn on the console and the computer.

The computer instantly recognizes new memory when the PC next
starts up.

You may see an error message. Relax! This is normal. Follow the onscreen instructions to adjust the PC's BIOS to update the new total
amount of memory. Save the changes. Then, restart the computer.
(Directions appear on the screen.)

I recommend using the online Web site www.crucial.com for buying new memory for your computer. When you know the computer's make and model, you can work the "memory configurator" on that Web site and figure out exactly how much of what kind of memory your computer needs. It may not be the least expensive memory on the Internet, but the service and support make the price worth it.

Adding more memory may trigger Windows XP to yearn for reactivation. See also "Adding New Hardware."

# Removing Memory

It's best to install computer memory into open or available memory slots. Then again, you probably weren't thinking about upgrading when you first bought your PC, so all the memory banks are full. To add new memory, you need to remove all or some of the old memory. Here's how to yank out those memory DIMMs:

*1.* Turn off and unplug the PC's console.

Keep the plug well away from the console, in case it suddenly becomes animated and desires to plug itself in again under its own power.

*2.* Open the PC's console.

Lay aside that can opener: Use a screwdriver to remove screws from the rear of the case. Note that some newer PC cases don't have screws and it's quite easy to open the console.

*3.* Locate the memory banks.

They're found on the motherboard in groups of two or four.

*4.* Push aside the clips on the short ends of the memory card or DIMM.

The clips keep the DIMM snug in its socket. By pushing them aside, you free up the DIMM. Notice that the DIMM is pushed up a tad out of its socket. Handy.

*5.* Set the DIMM aside.

*6.* Proceed with installing any new memory, as covered in the preceding section.

There's little value in old computer memory. You can try to sell it on eBay, if you like. I don't recommend throwing it out; instead, keep it in a safe, dry place where it won't get stepped on or come into contact with any metal or anything that can cause sparks or static electricity.

If you do plan on selling the old memory on eBay, repackage it in the container that your new memory came in. That keeps it safe for shipping.

# Removing USB Storage Devices

Although you can easily attach and remove USB devices, those USB storage devices must be properly removed, or ejected, by Windows. Failure to do so properly may result in missing or damaged files.

To properly remove the device, locate the Safely Remove Hardware icon in the system tray. Click that icon.

Choose the removable USB device from the pop-up list; click it with the mouse.

When the computer tells you that it's okay to remove the disk or device, you can do so.

If the disk is in use, meaning that there are open files on the disk or programs using the disk, you see a warning dialog box. Click the Cancel button in that case.

Removable USB devices include flash memory drives; media cards; external hard drives and CD-ROM/DVD drives; and any other USB device that is used to store information. You can see the lot listed in the My Computer window.

# Software Installation and Removal

For the most part, adding new software to your computer is cinchy: Simply insert the new software's CD or DVD disc into the CD or DVD drive. Installation should proceed automatically after that; follow the instructions or directions on the computer screen.

When inserting the disk does nothing, which is always the case with software that comes on a floppy disk, you need to manually run the Install or Setup program. The easiest way to do that is by using the Control Panel's Add or Remove Programs icon. See also "The Add or Remove Programs Icon."

## Installing software you downloaded from the Internet

Programs downloaded from the Internet come in one of two types: EXE, or program files that install automatically, or ZIP files, which you must decompress and then install.

Installing an EXE file is easy: Simply locate the downloaded file by using Windows Explorer. Double-click to open and run the program file. Obey the instructions on the screen.

Most downloaded programs don't come in the EXE format, which is sad. The main reason is to protect against viruses; you shouldn't wantonly download EXE program files.

To install software from a ZIP file, you must first remove the files from the zip archive and then run any special Install or Setup program. These steps overview the operation:

*1.* Locate the downloaded ZIP file.

In Windows XP, ZIP files appear as compressed folders. The icon is shown in the margin. If you've installed special ZIP file-management software, such as WinZip, that ZIP file icon is used instead.

*2.* Open the downloaded ZIP file folder.

*3.* In the panel on the left side of the window, in the Folder Tasks area, choose Extract All Files.

The Extraction Wizard starts.

*4.* Click the Next button once, and then click it again. Then click the Finish button.

After you complete these steps, a new folder is created. The new folder shares the same name as the compressed folder, but it's not a compressed folder. The new folder's window opens immediately after you click the Finish button, which saves you lotsa steps.

*5.* Locate the installation program, named either Setup or Install.

At this point, installation should proceed as it would for any program you install in Windows.

When there's no Setup or Install program, you have to see the downloaded program's instructions for further information. Try to find a file named Readme or Readme.Doc. Open that file for more instructions.

I recommend keeping the original ZIP or EXE file so that you can reinstall the program later, if you desire. You can delete the extra folder that's created by extracting files from the zip (compressed folder) archive (refer to Step 4).

## Uninstalling software

Removing software is much easier now than it was in the old days. Even so, you must use the proper methods for removing a program.

The first thing to try is to visit the Add or Remove Programs icon in the Control Panel. Locate the program on the list and click the Remove button to properly uninstall the program. See also "The Add or Remove Programs Icon."

The second thing to try is to locate the program's submenu entry on the Start button's Programs menu. Usually included on the program's submenu is an Uninstall option.

The last thing you want to do is manually delete the program from your computer. Although that rids you of the program's main file, it doesn't completely uninstall the program. Remnants and pieces of the program continue to lurk on your computer's hard drive and eventually cause you much woe. Because of that, I don't recommend manually deleting programs.

# Part III

# *The On–Off Thing*

Some devices run all the time — a refrigerator, for example. Other devices must be turned on and off, which is done easily by using a common switch: The toaster's large handle turns the thing on and automatically turns it off after producing toast of the desired toastiness. The oven, the dishwasher, the dryer, and other devices have dials and timers to turn themselves on and off. The water heater heats water automatically and turns itself on and off as needed.

With a computer, you can just toss out the window all the on–off knowledge you've gained throughout your life. Although nothing could be simpler than flipping a light switch, few things in this life are as complex as turning a computer on — and fewer things are more daunting than turning the blasted computer off!

## In this part . . .

## Changing the Power Button's Function

It's not an on–off switch any more. No, it's a *power button*. That's because you can change its function and make the computer do different things when you press that button. Here's how to set the power button's function just so:

*1.* Open the Control Panel.

You can get there from the Start button's menu; choose the Control Panel item.

 *2.* Open the Power Options icon.

*3.* Click the Advanced tab.

The drop-down list in the Power Buttons area controls the PC's power button behavior. You may see as many as five options, depending on what your PC's hardware is capable of:

- **Ask me what to do.** Pressing the power button displays the Turn Off Computer dialog box, where you can choose various options for shutting down the computer, entering Stand By mode, Hibernating, and so forth.

- **Do nothing.** Pressing the power button doesn't do squat.

- **Hibernate.** The computer enters hibernation mode.

- **Shut down.** The computer shuts down.

- **Stand by.** The computer enters Stand By (sleep or suspended) mode.

*4.* Select an option from the list to indicate what you want the power button to do.

*5.* Click OK.

Normally, pressing the power button causes Windows to shut down (see also "Turning the Computer System Off").

See also the next section.

## Forcing the Computer Off

After you've abandoned all hope of properly shutting down your PC, you can try this one simple trick to turn the thing off: Press and hold the power button. Keep holding it for about five seconds or so. Eventually, the console turns off.

Well, you can also try unplugging the thing or turning off the UPS. Nothing wrong with that — as long as the computer *is* locked up and you have tried properly shutting down first.

# *Hibernation*

As an alternative to turning your computer off, you can use the faster Hibernation option. What it does is to save the PC's current state: the open files, information in memory, and all that stuff. Then the computer is turned off, like a bear sleeping out the winter in a cave. The next time you turn the computer on, it starts up and loads everything back into memory, and you're ready to go.

Unlike turning the computer off, when the PC hibernates, open programs and files stay open. In fact, it's as though nothing was really shut down; the computer saves and restores everything. So, after you log on, your computer is just as you left it.

To hibernate your computer, follow these steps:

*1.* Click the Start button.

*2.* From the Start menu, choose the item labeled Turn Off Computer.

Look in the lower-right corner of the Start menu.

The Turn Off Computer window appears.

*3.* Press the Shift key on the keyboard.

Either Shift key works. Note that the Stand By button changes its label to read *Hibernate*. Keep the Shift key down!

*4.* Click the Hibernate button.

You can release the Shift key now.

The computer turns itself off. But, unlike in a normal shutdown, you're not prompted to save things or close programs. Instead, everything is saved to disk and the system shuts down.

To unhibernate, just turn the computer on as you normally would. The system revives from Hibernation mode and returns to the way it was before you hibernated, open programs and everything.

Not every computer has the Hibernation option. If pressing the Shift key in Step 3 doesn't change the Turn off Computer window, your PC cannot be put into hibernation.

If you're required to log on to Windows, you have to log on after the computer starts again, just as you do when you first turn on the PC.

You can configure the computer to automatically hibernate after a given period of inactivity. See also "Automatically going into Stand By mode." The instructions there also apply to hibernation.

# Logging On and Off

Windows requires you to identify yourself properly before you can use the PC. This is true for most computer operating systems. It's done for security reasons, to ensure that you are who you say you are. That way, you and only you can access your own files. Also, the computer can remember any personal settings or foofoo you've set up inside Windows.

*Log,* or *logging,* is an ugly term, but it's the most accurate. The term *log* goes back years. It helps to think of a ship's log, where the captain would write down information about the vessel and its travels. For a computer, a user must log in to identify himself to the system.

*Log in* and *log on* mean the same thing: to identify yourself to the computer system.

*Log off* is the term that's used when you're done with the computer and sign out for the day.

A *login* is the name you use to identify yourself to the computer system. This unique name identifies you and your account on that PC.

*Log on* is a verb, meaning to log on or log in to a computer system.

Logging on and off are necessary for security, but useful only when more than one person is using the same computer.

## Logging in

To log in to Windows XP, click the picture or name associated with your account. Optionally, type a password, and then press Enter.

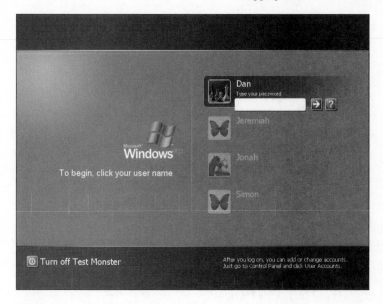

After a few moments, Windows completes its startup and you can begin using the computer.

## Logging off

To log off Windows, obey these steps:

*1.* Click the Start button.

*2.* Click the Log Off button.

It's down toward the lower center of the Start menu.

Windows desires to know whether you want to log off or just switch users.

*3.* Click the Log Off button.

Windows proceeds just as it would for shutting down the computer, but rather than complete the job, it merely pauses and redisplays the logon screen while it waits for someone else to use the computer.

If you choose the Switch User option (in Step 3), Windows doesn't bother to shut down your programs. Instead, those programs and windows stay open, and Windows merely allows another user to log in at that point. The other user who logs in can work on the PC, but Windows still remembers what the first user was doing.

By switching users, you can have one person quickly use the computer while the other waits. This saves time over logging out all the way or turning the computer off and then on again.

You don't need to log off the computer if you're done for the day. Instead, simply shut down Windows or hibernate the computer.

## Quitting Windows

When you're done using Windows, you need to quit, or shut down, the operating system. Because Windows is the same program that runs the computer, quitting Windows is the same thing as turning the computer off. In fact, on modern PCs, quitting Windows also turns off the console. (But it doesn't turn off the rest of the computer system; see also "Turning the Computer System Off.")

To quit Windows, pursue these steps:

*1.* Save your stuff! Close open programs!

Windows prompts you to save if you forget, but I recommend starting out the shutdown procedure by saving and closing first.

*2.* Click the Start button.

*3.* From the Start menu, choose the item labeled Turn Off Computer.

The Turn Off Computer window appears.

*4.* Click the Turn Off button.

The computer shuts itself down.

Modern PCs go so far as to turn off the console as well. For turning off additional things, see "Turning the Computer System Off."

If the computer immediately restarts, you have a problem — typically, a hardware problem. Refer to my book *Troubleshooting Your PC For Dummies* (Wiley Publishing, Inc.) for more information.

## *Restarting Windows*

Sometimes, it's necessary to start over again with a clean slate. For example, after installing some new hardware or new software or performing a Windows update, it's necessary to restart Windows. Here's how it's done:

*1.* Click the Start button.

*2.* Choose the item Turn Off Computer.

It's located in the lower-right part of the Start menu.

Selecting the Turn Off Computer item doesn't turn off the computer. Instead, it displays a Turn Off Computer window.

*3.* Choose Restart from the Turn Off Computer menu.

Windows begins shutting down, and then the computer restarts.

If any unsaved documents are open, you're prompted to save them before the computer restarts.

The keyboard shortcut for restarting Windows is Win, U, R. For keyboards without a Windows key, use Ctrl+Esc, U, R.

Restarting Windows is just like turning the computer off and on again, though you don't need to use the power button. The computer shuts down and closes all programs and, eventually, Windows itself. Then, the computer immediately restarts, just as though it were turned on.

Restarting Windows can also be referred to as *resetting* the computer.

Old-timers refer to restarting Windows as a *warm boot*.

If your console sports a Reset button, don't use it to restart Windows. Follow the instructions in this section instead.

## *Stand By Mode*

All modern PCs are equipped with energy-saving hardware and software. One of the energy-saving features gives the computer the ability to go to sleep, or to be put into Stand By mode where the computer is still on but consumes less power.

You can configure your PC to enter Stand By mode after a given period of inactivity, immediately, or never, depending on your whim and how much you enjoy saving energy.

Stand By mode is also known as Suspended mode or Sleep mode.

## Putting your PC into Stand By mode

To manually put the computer into Stand By mode, follow these steps:

*1.* Click the Start button.

*2.* Choose the item Turn Off Computer.

*3.* Choose Stand By from the Turn Off Computer menu.

The computer enters its power-saving mode.

The screen goes dark, and you may hear the hard drive warble down to a stop. The computer is asleep. Shhhh!

The computer isn't really totally turned off (not like Hibernation mode). Some functions are still working. But most of the power-draining things that the computer does are halted.

## Automatically going into Stand By mode

You can configure the PC to automatically enter Stand By mode after a period of inactivity, such as an hour or so after any key on the keyboard was pressed or the mouse was moved. The Power Options icon in the Control Panel is where you need to go:

*1.* Open the Control Panel.

 *2.* Open the Power Options icon.

The Stand By options are listed in the lower part of the Power Schemes tab. There are separate settings for the hard monitor and hard drive as well as for the entire system.

3. Set a timeout value for the monitor.

   After that period of inactivity, the PC's display adapter stops sending a signal, which places the computer's monitor into Sleep mode.

4. Set a timeout value for the hard disks.

   After the specified period of inactivity occurs, the computer powers down the hard drives.

5. Set a timeout value for the entire system to enter Stand By mode.

   This value overrides the individual settings for the monitor and hard drives.

6. Click OK to lock in your settings.

   Optionally, close the Control Panel window as well.

I don't recommend setting a timeout for your computer's hard drives. Doing so makes the computer act sluggish because it takes a while for the hard drives to spin back up to speed.

If you're using a screen saver, note that the timeout value for the monitor in Stand By mode overrides the screen saver's timeout setting. For example, if the screen saver comes on after 45 minutes but the monitor goes into Stand By mode after 30 minutes, you never see your screen saver.

## Waking up from Stand By mode

To rouse the computer from its Stand By mode slumber, press any key on the keyboard or jiggle the mouse. The computer wakes up after a moment.

The best "any key" to press is the Ctrl key on the keyboard.

If the PC doesn't wake up, it may have gone comatose. This happens sometimes; PCs can crash in their sleep. See also "Forcing the Computer Off." See also *Troubleshooting Your PC For Dummies*, which I wrote (Wiley Publishing, Inc.).

# Turning the Computer System Off

If you want to be good to your PC, and have your computer system last a good long time, pay attention to shutting it down properly. Too many people ignore this good advice, and their PCs suffer for it. Don't be one of them. Instead, turn off your computer system like this:

1. Quit Windows.

   See also "Quitting Windows."

2. Turn off the console if it doesn't turn itself off automatically.

3. Turn off the monitor plus any other peripherals attached to the PC.

You're done. Walk away.

The key is to turn off the console first and then turn off other things connected to the console: the monitor, printer, scanner, and external disk drives.

Not every external device has a power switch; some external disk drives and scanners have no on–off switch. Just let them be.

If everything is plugged into a power strip, you can turn off everything by turning off the power strip.

Likewise, you can turn off things by turning off the UPS. (But don't unplug the UPS because that could run down the battery.)

The worst thing to do is simply unplug the computer to turn it off. Sometimes that's necessary in instances of dire need. But don't make it a habit.

## Turning the Computer System On

The best way to turn on your computer system is in this order:

1. Turn on the computer's peripherals first: monitor, printer, external disk drives, and scanner, for example.

2. Turn on the console last.

The reason for turning on the console last is that it's in charge. If everything else is on and up to speed, the console can easily and quickly recognize it. Otherwise, for example, if you neglect to turn on an external hard drive, the computer doesn't recognize it right way (though modern PCs recognize an external hard drive whenever you turn the drive on).

If you're using a power strip or UPS, the procedure works the same: peripherals first and then the console, though it really doesn't matter if everything is turned on all at once.

After the computer comes to life, you need to log in to Windows. See also "Logging On and Off."

# The Uninterruptible Power Supply

One of the best things you can buy for your PC is a UPS, or uninterruptible *power* supply. That's a gizmo that's essentially a large battery inside a power strip. The battery supplies power so that any gizmos plugged into the UPS don't suffer instant death after a power outage.

Many UPSs are also equipped with special electronic filters and noise protection, which further insulates your delicate electronic equipment from various electrical evils.

Connect only the console and the monitor to the UPS. Specifically, connect them to the battery-backed-up sockets on the UPS. You can connect your other peripherals to the non-battery-backed-up sockets or to a regular power strip.

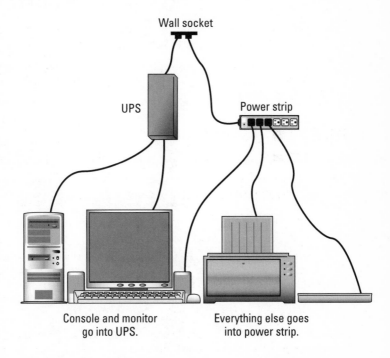

Wall socket

UPS

Power strip

Console and monitor
go into UPS.

Everything else goes
into power strip.

The idea here is to keep the console and monitor active during a power emergency. That way, you can save your stuff and properly shut down. Printing, scanning, and using the Internet can wait until the power comes back on.

You can get a UPS at any office supply or computer store. They're rated by how long they can keep things going after a power outage, and also by how many sockets they have, how many are battery-powered, and other features.

Note that having a UPS isn't your ticket to computing in the dark. When the power goes out, you should immediately save your stuff and shut down the computer safely and properly.

The UPS beeps when there's a power disruption or beeps constantly when the power is out. That's your signal to save your stuff, quit Windows, and shut down the PC.

The time rating on a UPS is for comparison purposes only. In my experience, most UPS batteries give up only a few minutes after the power goes out — even though the UPS may be rated for 30 or 45 minutes. Be safe: Save your stuff, power down, turn off. Wait for the power to come back on. (Go read a book . . . by candlelight!)

# Popular Places in Windows

Windows covers a vast expanse of territory. It has to. A computer's operating system has many tasks, duties, and responsibilities. To avoid chaos and confusion, Windows itself is composed of many smaller locales — like outposts on the territory. These are places you may visit all the time to do common things, or locations you may not need to visit that often. Regardless, those places exist, and they help you and Windows keep your computer system alive and happy.

## In this part ...

All Programs Menu

Control Panel

Desktop

My Computer

My Documents

My Network Places

Recycle Bin

Start Button

System Tray

Taskbar

## All Programs Menu

Software installed on your computer can be accessed through the All Programs menu. That's where you can go to start just about any program installed on your computer.

Here's how you can access the All Programs menu:

1. Click the Start button.

   This step pops up the Start menu.

2. Choose All Programs.

   The All Programs main menu is displayed.

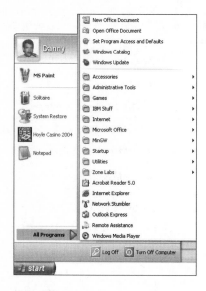

From the menu, you can choose a program to run.

Selecting a submenu displays that submenu's contents, from which you can choose a program or select yet another submenu to peruse.

Not all programs are listed on the All Programs menu. Some of the more obscure Windows utilities aren't listed. Some programs you download from the Internet aren't listed either.

The keyboard shortcut to access the All Programs menu is Win, P, Enter. If your keyboard lacks a Win (Windows) key, try Ctrl+Esc, P, Enter. Use the keyboard's arrow keys to navigate the menus; press Enter to select and run a command.

If you're using Windows XP in the "classic" visual mode, the name of the menu is Programs and not All Programs.

## Starting a program

You use the All Programs menu to start a program. For example, to start the Notepad text editor, follow these steps:

*1.* Click the Start button to display the Start menu.

*2.* Choose All Programs.

*3.* Choose Accessories.

*4.* Choose Notepad.

The Notepad program starts and opens its window.

These instructions can also be written this way:

*1.* Click the Start button to display the Start menu.

*2.* Choose All Programs⇨Accessories⇨Notepad.

The Notepad program starts and opens its window.

You can close Notepad: Choose File⇨Exit from its menu.

## Popular menus on the All Programs menu

Windows preconfigures a few submenus on the All Programs menu, places you may find yourself visiting from time to time. Here are a few of the more popular All Programs submenus and what you may find there:

**Games:** This is where the Windows games are! Note, though, that other games are installed on their own, separate submenus (usually named after the game developer or distributor).

**Accessories:** Many of the smaller Windows assistant programs appear on the Accessories menu: Calculator, Command Prompt, Notepad, Paint, Windows Explorer, and WordPad are among the more popular.

**Accessories⇨System Tools:** This sub-submenu contains lots of handy Windows utilities and programs, including Backup, Disk Cleanup, Disk Defragmenter, and System Restore.

## The Startup submenu

A special menu on the All Programs menu is named Startup. Any programs placed on this submenu start automatically when Windows starts.

Some applications automatically put their programs on the Startup submenu when they're installed.

To prevent a program from starting, move it from the Startup submenu to another submenu. Just drag the item with the mouse or edit the menu (see also "Organizing the All Programs menu").

## Creating a desktop shortcut to a program

Navigating the menus and submenus of the All Programs menu can be tricky. For programs you use often, consider creating a desktop shortcut icon to the program instead of having to use the All Programs menu.

To copy a program from the All Programs menu to a shortcut icon on the desktop, follow these steps:

*1.* Click the Start button to display the Start menu.

*2.* Choose All Programs and find your program on the menu.

For example, choose Accessories and then locate WordPad.

*3.* Right-click the program's command.

So, rather than left-click the command, which would start the program, you right-click. This step displays a pop-up menu.

*4.* Choose Send To➪Desktop (create shortcut).

The program's icon appears on the desktop as a shortcut file.

*5.* Press the Esc key on the keyboard to back up out of the submenus and hide any menus that are displayed.

The shortcut icon on the desktop can be double-clicked to run the program. Many PC users find this easier than wading through the All Programs menu. But do this trick for only those programs you use most often, lest the desktop get cluttered.

See also Part VI for information on shortcut icons.

## Organizing the All Programs menu

Just about any new program you install creates its own menu on the All Programs menu. This leads to a messy situation after a while. I've seen some All Programs menus that are so tall they cannot fit on the screen. That's not very organized.

You can organize programs and menus on the All Programs menu easily. The idea is to create main folders and then organize the programs and submenus into those folders.

As an example, here are some ideas for the main folders on the All Programs menu:

- ✔ Internet
- ✔ Utilities
- ✔ Games
- ✔ Microsoft Office
- ✔ Accessories
- ✔ Misc

There's no definitive list; you can create and use whichever folders you believe would best keep you organized.

To do the organization, you need to move around the various existing menus and commands. Right-click the Start button and choose Open from the pop-up menu. Creating and arranging the items is done in a manner similar to managing folders. See also Part VII. (Remember that folders are submenus and that shortcut icons are commands.)

# Control Panel

Windows uses a central location, called the Control Panel, to help you manage many aspects of your computer. Most hardware adjustments and modifications take place by using one of the many icons appearing on the Control Panel.

To display the Control Panel, click the Start button and choose Control Panel from the menu.

You can also see the Control Panel from any Windows Explorer window: Click the down arrow on the Address bar and select Control Panel from the list.

In Windows XP, the Control Panel has two modes of operation: Classic and Category. Classic view displays all the icons in one window.

Category view displays only the most popular icons. Other icons are accessed in subcategories.

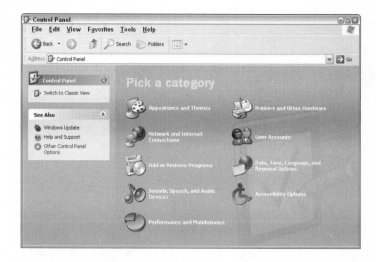

To change views, use the task pane, on the left side of the window, in the Control Panel area.

If the Control Panel isn't available as an item on the Start menu, follow these steps to make it so:

*1.* Right-click the Start button.

2. Choose Properties from the pop-up menu.

3. In the Taskbar and Start Menu Properties dialog box, click the Customize button.

   The Customize Start Menu dialog box appears.

4. Click the Advanced tab.

5. Locate Control Panel on the scrolling list.

   It should be the first item.

6. Choose the option below Control Panel that reads Display As a Link.

7. Click OK to close the various open dialog boxes.

The Control Panel now appears as a command on the main Start menu.

To make the Control Panel appear as a menu, with its icons showing up as submenu commands, choose the option Display As a Menu in Step 6.

## Desktop

The *desktop* is the main interface Windows provides. It's what you see when you first start Windows — home plate, as it were.

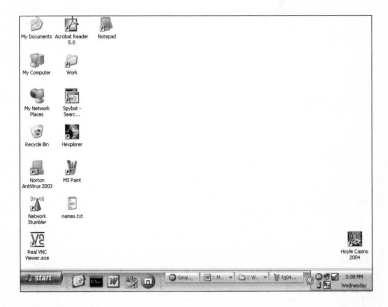

The desktop is where various program windows appear as you use Windows.

The desktop is also home to numerous icons. The icons are considered to be "on the desktop." That keeps them handy.

The desktop can have a background, or *wallpaper,* image, or it can be a solid color. You make that choice in the Display Properties dialog box, on the Desktop tab.

Summon the Display Properties dialog box by right-clicking the desktop and choosing Properties from the pop-up menu. (Right-click the desktop, or background, not an icon on the desktop.)

The size of the desktop can be adjusted in the Display Properties dialog box as well, on the Settings tab.

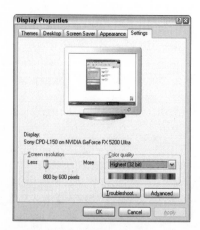

The taskbar appears on the desktop, though it's not a part of the desktop. (See also "Taskbar.")

The term *desktop* has little to do with the thing today. On an older computer, the desktop appeared as a graphical representation of a desktop, complete with a pad of paper, a calendar, a glue pot, scissors, and other items commonly found on a real desktop.

# My Computer

My Computer is the name of an icon and a window where information about your computer and its storage devices can be found.

 To access the My Computer window, open the My Computer icon on the desktop. The My Computer window lists the stuff that exists inside your computer, primarily the disk drives but also any digital cameras or scanners attached to your computer.

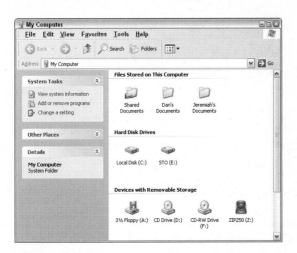

You can also access the My Computer window by choosing My Computer from the Address bar's drop-down list in any Windows Explorer window.

The My Computer window may also be available as a command on the Start button's menu.

This window is often used as a starting place when navigating through various disk drives and when file hunting.

The My Computer window allows you to quickly access information about your computer's disk drives. Right-clicking a drive and choosing the Properties command displays information about that drive.

You can eject removable disks in the My Computer window. Click to select a disk, and then choose File⇨Eject from the menu.

# My Documents

My Documents is the name of an icon that appears on the desktop, as well as the name of the folder that the icon represents. The folder is the home for all the documents, files, and whatnot you create on your computer. Indeed, it's a home for *your* documents.

 To view the contents of the My Documents folder, open the My Documents icon the desktop. The contents of the window list any files you've created or saved in that folder:

You may also see other folders in the My Documents folder window, such as the My Music and My Pictures folders, which are used in Windows and by various applications to store music and graphics files, respectively.

Other folders in the window are created to help keep your stuff organized. (See also Part VII.)

You can get to the My Documents folder from the Address bar in any Windows Explorer window: Select the Address bar and choose My Documents from the drop-down list.

There may be a command to open the My Documents folder on the Start button's menu as well.

Each user on the PC has his own My Documents menu. What you see in Windows as My Documents is unique for your own account. When another user logs on to Windows, he has his own, distinct My Documents folder and does not see or have access to the files in your account's My Documents folder or its contents.

# My Network Places

My Network Places is the name of an icon on the desktop that opens a window listing various locations on the local network or the Internet.

 Opening the My Network Places icon reveals a window that lists any shared folders or resources on other computers on the local network — if any.

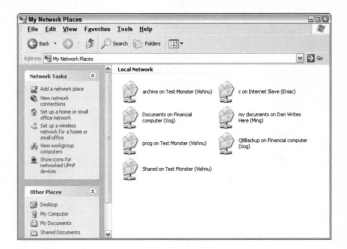

Opening the folders listed in the My Network Places window allows you to access files on other computers.

You can also access this window by choosing My Network Places from the drop-down list on any Address bar in any folder's window.

The My Network Places window may also be available from a My Network Places command on the main Start menu.

The My Network Places icon may appear on the desktop, even if your computer isn't on a local-area network. The icon's appearance is optional. You can remove the icon by following these steps:

*1.* Open the Control Panel.

See also "Control Panel."

2. Open the Display icon.

3. In the Display Properties dialog box, click the Desktop tab.

4. Click the Customize Desktop button.

The Desktop Items dialog box appears.

5. Click to remove the check mark by My Network Places.

Removing the check mark removes that item from the desktop.

 Likewise, you can remove check marks by other icons (My Documents, My Computer, Internet Explorer) to remove those icons from the desktop.

6. Click OK when you're done.

7. Click OK in the Display Properties dialog box as well.

You can also close the Control Panel if you're done with it.

## Recycle Bin

The *Recycle Bin* is a storage location for files you delete on your computer. It's there because many folks often delete files and then change their minds. By storing those "deleted" files in the Recycle Bin, Windows gives you a chance to recover the files later.

 Opening the Recycle Bin icon on the desktop displays the contents of the Recycle Bin folder, a collection of all the files you've deleted on your computer.

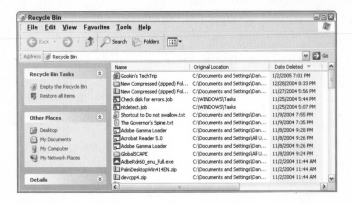

To see the most recently deleted files listed first, choose View⇨ Arrange Icons By⇨Date Deleted from the menu.

Files stay in the Recycle Bin until they're removed. Files are removed automatically over time as the Recycle Bin is being used. You can also manually remove or empty the Recycle Bin.

Removing files from the Recycle Bin helps improve the amount of disk storage space available. But, sadly, removing files from the Recycle Bin means that there's no way to recover them if you want them.

# Start Button

The Start button is the key you turn to start just about anything in Windows: programs, activities, adjustments, fine-tuning — even stopping the computer is done through the power of the Start button.

The Start button lives on one end of the taskbar. Normally, the taskbar sits on the bottom of the screen (though it can be moved), and the Start button dwells in the screen's lower-left corner.

Activating the Start button pops up the Start menu. You can acti-vate the Start button by clicking it with the mouse. Or, you can press the Win key on the keyboard, which also pops up the Start button's menu.

If your keyboard lacks a Win key, pressing the Ctrl+Esc key combi-nation pops up the Start button's menu.

Press the Esc key, or Win key, to make the Start button's menu go away.

## Start button menu

The Start button's menu contains many shortcuts for getting to other places in Windows, as well as accessing commonly used programs and the powerful All Programs menu.

The top of the menu lists your user ID and picture. (Windows refers to the logon ID or login ID as a *user ID.*)

You can change the picture by clicking it with the mouse. That opens the User Accounts icon from the Control Panel, where user accounts are messed with.

The left side of the Start menu lists popular programs. The top half of the menu is the *pin-on* area, where certain popular programs can be placed. The bottom part of the left side lists recently used programs.

The right side of the Start menu contains three different areas. At the top are popular places and folders to visit in Windows. The middle contains places to visit for changing settings in Windows. The bottom area is for help and other commands.

## Changing the Start menu's look

There are two ways to view the Start menu in Windows: the new way and the boring classic way. To choose one or the other, follow these steps:

*1.* Right-click the Start button.

*2.* Choose Properties from the pop-up menu.

The Taskbar and Start Menu Properties dialog box appears, with the Start Menu tab forward.

*3.* Choose Classic Start Menu.

You can preview in the dialog box what the classic Start menu looks like. It's more reminiscent of the old Windows 98/Me/2000 Start menu. Boring.

*4.* Click OK to change the Start menu, or click the Cancel button to keep it as is.

## Adding or removing items from the Start button menu

The Start button's menu is customizable. You can change just about any aspect of the menu, from what appears and how it appears to where specific things go. To wield such might, mind these steps:

*1.* Right-click the Start button.

*2.* Choose Properties from the pop-up menu.

I assume that you're using the Windows XP Start menu and not the Classic Start menu.

*3.* Click the Customize button.

The Customize Start Menu dialog box lets you control what does and what doesn't show up on the Start button's menu.

The General tab controls how many programs appear on the recently used programs list (on the left side of the menu, at the bottom).

4. Click the Advanced tab.

   The Advanced tab contains a scrolling list of items you can select to display or not display on the right side of the Start menu.

5. Click the OK button after making your choices.

   Close any other open dialog boxes or windows.

I call the upper-left part of the Start button's menu the "pin-on" area. You can attach any program icon to this area by right-clicking that icon and choosing the Pin to Start Menu command.

Icons can be removed from the pin-on area by right-clicking them and choosing the Unpin from Start Menu command from the pop-up menu.

# System Tray

The system tray sits on the opposite end of the taskbar from the Start menu. If the taskbar is on the bottom of the screen, the system tray is on the right side of the taskbar.

The system tray normally displays the time of day as well as the day of the week.

You may also see a volume control on the system tray.

The system tray also displays other icons. Those icons represent various running tasks or programs, many of which monitor things that go on in the computer "in the background." For example, an antivirus program may have its icon appear on the system tray.

Icons on the system tray may display messages from time to time that alert you to certain changing conditions in the computer.

You can control the icons on the system tray by using the mouse. Clicking, double-clicking, or right-clicking the icons controls their behavior, making them pop up a menu, display a window, or do something else (though some icons don't do anything). Sometimes, merely pointing the mouse at an icon does the job. What the icon does, of course, depends on which program the icon represents.

The system tray is also known as the *notification area,* though most manuals and documentation refer to it as the system tray.

You can eliminate many of the things displayed on the system tray, but you cannot fully eliminate the system tray from the taskbar.

## Displaying the time on the system tray

You can turn the time display on or off by following these steps:

1. Right-click the time display on the system tray.

2. Choose Properties from the pop-up menu.

3. In the Taskbar and Start Menu Properties dialog box, locate the Show the Clock item.

4. Remove the check mark to hide the clock display; place a check mark in the box to show the clock.

5. Click OK.

## Displaying the volume icon on the system tray

The volume icon is displayed on the system tray courtesy of the Control Panel's Sounds and Audio Devices icon. Here's how to turn that display off or on:

1. Open the Control Panel.

 2. Open the Sounds and Audio Devices icon.

3. On the Volume tab, locate the item labeled Place Volume Icon in the Taskbar.

4. Place or remove the check mark to show or hide the volume display on the system tray.

5. Click OK to close the dialog box.

You can optionally close the Control Panel's window as well.

## Controlling the visibility of system tray icons

You can elect to show or hide some or all of the icons on the system tray. Your first tool is the Show/Hide chevron, located on the left end of the system tray. To show all the icons, click that button when it's pointing left.

Click the button when it's pointing right to hide some or all of the icons.

If you would rather show all the icons all the time, follow these steps:

1. Right-click a blank spot on the system tray.

Or, you can right-click the time.

2. Choose Properties from the pop-up menu.

The Taskbar and Start Menu Properties dialog box is displayed.

*3.* Remove the check mark by the item Hide Inactive Icons.

*4.* Click OK.

The taskbar now shows all its icons.

Notice that the Show/Hide chevron is missing. To reenter that mode, repeat the preceding steps and replace the check mark in Step 3 (rather than remove it).

You can also control which icons individually appear or hide. Here's how:

*1.* Right-click a blank spot on the system tray.

*2.* From the pop-up menu, choose the command named Customize Notifications.

If you don't see this command or it appears dimmed, you must repeat the preceding set of steps to hide inactive items on the system tray. Otherwise, the Customize Notifications dialog box appears.

*3.* Click to select the name of an icon that you want to either hide or display all the time.

After you select the name, the text in the Behavior column changes to a drop-down menu.

*4.* Use the Behavior drop-down menu to select how the icon is displayed.

You have three options:

- **Hide when inactive:** The icon shows up when its program is being used or when the icon thinks that it's active.

- **Always hide:** The icon is always hidden.

- **Always show:** The icon is always shown.

**5.** Repeat Step 4 for each icon you want to control.

**6.** Click the OK button when you're done showing or hiding individual icons.

Note that changing how individual icons show up may or may not work for all the teensy icons on the system tray.

# Taskbar

The taskbar exists as a strip, usually found along the bottom of the desktop (though it can move). On the left end of the taskbar is the Start button. The right end of the taskbar is the system tray.

In the middle, the taskbar displays buttons, one for each running program or open window on the desktop.

Clicking a button on the taskbar instantly switches attention to that button's window and brings the window up front and ready for action. Other windows, if any, are shuffled behind the open window. The open window is then said to be "on top."

The taskbar is also host to various toolbars, which appear on the taskbar between the Start button and system tray. Yes, it's possible for the taskbar to be a very crowded place.

## Moving the taskbar

The taskbar can be relocated to any edge of the screen: top, bottom, right, or left. Here's how to move the taskbar:

**1.** Point the mouse at a blank part of the taskbar.

Find a spot in the middle, away from other buttons or graphical whatnot.

**2.** Drag the mouse to another edge of the screen.

The taskbar doesn't move as much as it "snaps" into position when you have the mouse pointer in the proper location.

3. Release the mouse button to drop the taskbar into its new position.

Be aware that most documentation assumes that the taskbar is at the *bottom* of the screen. That affects the position of the Start button and system tray.

You can use these instructions to move a wayward taskbar back to the bottom of the screen if it goes AWOL. (See also "Locking the taskbar.")

## Resizing the taskbar

The taskbar can be made fatter to accommodate more buttons, or made so thin as to be only a small line on the edge of the screen.

To resize the taskbar:

1. Position the mouse on the taskbar's outer edge, between the taskbar and the desktop.

   When you find the sweet spot, the mouse pointer changes to a this-way-that-way arrow (as shown in the margin).

2. Drag the mouse inward, toward the desktop, to make it thicker.

Or, drag the mouse outside, toward the edge of the screen, to make it thinner.

3. Release the mouse.

   The taskbar assumes the new size.

To prevent the taskbar's size from being changed, see the later section "Locking the taskbar."

## Automatically hiding the taskbar

You can elect to have the taskbar automatically shy away, to provide more room for windows on the desktop. This is known as the *Auto-hide* feature, and here's how you activate it:

1. Right-click the time in the system tray part of the taskbar.

2. Choose Properties from the pop-up menu.

This step displays the Taskbar and Start Menu Properties dialog box. The top part of the Taskbar tab deals with how the taskbar appears.

3. Click to put a check mark by the item labeled Auto-hide the Taskbar.

4. Click OK.

## Locking the taskbar

To prevent the taskbar from being moved or resized, you can lock it. This action not only prevents the taskbar from wandering to another edge of the screen, but also prevents you from moving or resizing any other toolbars on the taskbar. So, this may be an option you often turn off and on. Here's how:

1. Right-click the time in the system tray part of the taskbar.

2. Choose Properties from the pop-up menu.

3. Click to put a check mark by the item labeled Lock the Taskbar.

4. Click OK.

A locked taskbar has a slightly different look to it. It appears nar-rower; the top "lip" is missing. And, the dimple areas, used to move toolbars on the taskbar, disappear.

## Other toolbars

The taskbar is also home to other toolbars. In fact, you can stack the taskbar with an endless number of toolbars, which seems impractical, although it's possible.

Add a toolbar like this:

***1.*** Right-click a blank part of the taskbar.

Don't click a button or icon.

***2.*** Choose a new toolbar from the Toolbars submenu.

The number and variety of toolbars that appear depends on what features and applications you have installed in Windows.

After you choose a toolbar, the menu goes away and the new toolbar appears on the taskbar.

For example, adding the Address toolbar provides the taskbar with an Address text box, just like a Windows Explorer or Internet Explorer window.

You can type the name of a Web page to visit, or you can type the name of a program to run — all from the taskbar's Address toolbar.

Yes, adding toolbars can make the taskbar a busy place. See also "Moving a toolbar."

» When a toolbar is cut off and buttons or options are hidden, the toolbar grows a Show More button on its right end. Clicking this button (see the margin) displays the hidden toolbar options as a pop-up menu.

## Quick Launch bar

A special toolbar is the *Quick Launch* bar, which appears on most new Windows computers. This toolbar contains buttons showing icons that represent popular programs. To run a program, click the button. That's how the toolbar gets its name — clicking a button quickly launches that program.

To display the Quick Launch bar, follow these steps:

***1.*** Right-click the time in the system tray part of the taskbar.

***2.*** Choose Properties from the pop-up menu.

***3.*** Click to put a check mark by the item labeled Show Quick Launch.

***4.*** Click OK.

To add a new icon to the Quick Launch bar, simply drag a program's icon from the desktop or any window to the Quick Launch bar. (Note that this is a copy operation; the original icon isn't moved.)

To remove an icon from the Quick Launch bar, drag it up and to the desktop. That moves the icon to the desktop, and you can delete it from there.

You can also right-click an icon on the Quick Launch bar and choose the Delete command from the pop-up menu.

If you want to see smaller or larger icons on the Quick Launch bar, right-click the left end of the Quick Launch bar (on the dimple bar) and choose View⇨Large Icons or View⇨Small Icons from the pop-up menu.

## Moving a toolbar

Toolbars can be moved or rearranged, though it's not the easiest thing in the world to do.

First, the taskbar must *not* be locked.

Second, you must grab the toolbar by its left edge, on the *dimple bar*. Just point the mouse at the dimple bar — the mouse pointer spot.

Third, drag the toolbar either left, right, up, or down. Where you drag the toolbar depends on how big the taskbar is and how many other toolbars there are. It's really more of a trial-and-error thing; there are no solid or consistent instructions that can be relied on to move a toolbar.

Finally, when you have the toolbar positioned just right, let go of the mouse! The toolbar should stick where you left it. You can optionally lock the taskbar at this point.

Note that it's very easy to accidentally move toolbars on the taskbar.

## Removing a toolbar

The easiest way to zap a toolbar from the taskbar is to right-click its dimple bar area. This action produces a pop-up menu from which you can choose the Close Toolbar command.

If you don't see the Close Toolbar command on the pop-up menu, you've clicked in the wrong place. Try again.

Note that you cannot close the last toolbar, which is the taskbar itself (the part that displays the window buttons).

# Disk Drives

A computer is a creative tool. You use a computer to create or collect stuff. Applications and software programs on the computer help you to create stuff. You use the Internet to collect stuff that other folks create: pictures, videos, music, and other Web whatnot. You can include among all that stuff the programs you install and run on your computer. For all that stuff, the computer must have ample, reliable, and secure storage. On the PC, that storage is provided in the form of disk drives.

## In this part . . .

# About Disk Drives

As computers evolved, it became obvious to computer users and scientists that people didn't enjoy re-creating everything on a computer each time they turned the thing on. Yet, re-creating stuff was necessary because computers of the day had no long-term storage.

Now, things are different. Now, computers have long-term storage.

## Types of storage

Inside a computer are three types of storage, found in the microprocessor, RAM, and disk drives.

First, the microprocessor itself has some storage, but only a small amount, hardly enough to do anything more than basic math.

Second, the computer's RAM provides good storage, to supplement what the microprocessor has. Sadly, computer memory is temporary. Therefore, a third form of storage is needed, something long-term. That's the third form of storage: disk drives.

Disk drives are known as long-term storage.

Another term for disk storage is *disk memory*. Although technically accurate, the term *disk memory* is misleading; disk storage isn't memory, like RAM is.

## Saving and loading

To transfer information from memory to disk, you *save* that information. Indeed, the information is saved from the certain peril of short-term memory to the long-term safety of a disk drive.

To transfer information from a disk drive to memory, you *open* that information. (*Open* is the common term used in Windows, though some documentation uses the term *load* instead.)

# Bits and Bytes

Computer storage is measured by the byte, just as distances are measured in miles or kilometers — or inches or centimeters — and weight is measured by the ounce or gram. In computers, it's the byte.

A *byte* is a single character of information. The letter *A* can be stored in a byte, as can any letter, number, or symbol. For many bytes, common abbreviations are used, as described in this table:

| Name | Abbreviation | Characters (appx.) |
|------|-------------|--------------------|
| Byte | B | 1 |
| Kilobyte | KB | 1,000 |
| Megabyte | MB | 1 million |
| Gigabyte | GB | 1 billion |
| Terabyte | TB | 1 trillion |

# CD-ROM and DVD Drives

For high-capacity (meaning "lots of room") storage, your PC uses a CD-ROM or DVD drive, or sometimes one of each! These drives eat the shiny media, those 5-inch plastic discs. For your CD music player or DVD movie player, the discs contain music or videos, respectively. They can contain that information for your computer as well, but they can also contain data that the computer can use.

You can also use your computer to play music CDs or view DV videos.

CD-ROM stands for Compact Disc, Read-Only Memory. The CD-ROM drive reads CD-ROM discs. These discs cannot be written to; you cannot save information to a CD-ROM as you can to a hard drive. But the computer can read CD-ROM discs (hence, the *read-only* part of the acronym). Most new software you install on your PC comes on CD-ROM discs.

DVD stands for Digital Versatile Disc, or sometimes the V means Video. (The standards people called an early lunch before the exact acronym was agreed upon.) The drives read DVD-ROM discs, similar in appearance to CDs, but can store much more information. Otherwise, beyond the disc's capacity, a DVD drive is very similar to a CD drive on a computer.

DVD drives can also read (or *play*) CDs.

It's often hard to tell which drive is a CD or DVD drive. Generally speaking, CD drives have a CD logo on them, and DVD drives sport the DVD logo.

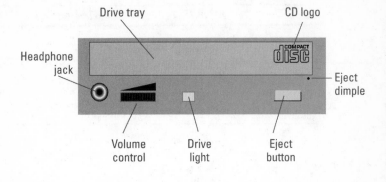

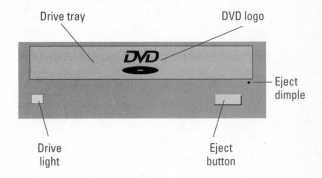

Note that CDs typically have a headphone jack and maybe a volume control, which DVDs lack.

CD-ROM or DVD discs may be referred to as CDs, DVDs, disks, or discs. Physically, all the discs look alike. Some discs may be labeled as CDs or DVDs, or you may see CD or DVD specified in the tiny text around the disc's center hole.

A typical computer CD stores anywhere from 650MB of data on up to about 720MB.

A typical computer DVD stores up to 4.7GB of information.

## Inserting a CD or DVD

CDs and DVDs are removable. They can be inserted or removed as needed.

Inserting a CD or DVD is done differently, depending on the design of the drive. There are two types: slot and tray.

✔ **Slot:** The drive has a narrow slot into which you insert the disc. About ⅓ to halfway in, the drive's mechanism grabs the disc and pulls it in the rest of the way.

✔ **Tray:** The disc sits in a tray that slides in and out of the drive. To extend the tray, press a button on the front of the drive. When the tray is fully extended, drop the disc into the round holding area atop the tray. When the disc is centered, push the button again to retract the tray.

 The button to extend or retract the tray is often labeled with the universal symbol for *eject,* as shown in the margin.

You can also retract the tray by gently pushing it back into the drive. Gently!

Discs are inserted label side up.

If the disc lacks a label, it may be double-sided. In any case, nothing bad happens when you insert the disc upside down. Just eject the disc, flip it over, and try again.

## Ejecting a CD or DVD

Removing a disc involves not only mechanically removing it, but also ensuring that Windows is done using the disc. You don't want to remove a disc that is in use; doing so causes various and ugly error messages to be displayed. It's embarrassing.

When you're done with a DVD or CD , eject it as follows:

1. Open the My Computer icon on the desktop.

2. Click to select the CD-ROM or DVD drive icon.

3. Choose File⇨Eject from the menu.

If the disc is still in use, Windows lets you know by displaying an error message. Heed that message to fix things (such as to quit a program or close an open program window). Then, try again.

Put the disc back into its protective envelope or container and store it in a proper place.

It's bad to leave discs lying about, where they can be scratched and damaged permanently.

For tray-type drives, you need to press the drive's Eject button to retract the tray after the computer ejects the disc.

 When the disc is stuck or the power is off and you need to eject it, use the dimple or small hole near the tray or insertion hole. Sticking a straightened paper clip into the hole and pushing gently pops the disc out of the drive.

## Playing a music CD or movie DVD

To play a musical CD or movie on a DVD, simply insert the disc into your computer's CD or DVD drive. The music or movie should play automatically. If not, see the next subsection.

To play a music CD or DVD, you need proper media software. On your PC, that software is provided by Windows Media Player, which is included with Windows — unless you live in a place where Microsoft has been sued over that, in which case you're free to choose your own media player.

## AutoPlay programs

When you insert a removable disc, it may automatically run a program, known as the AutoPlay program. For example, a CD containing a new program may run the Install or Setup procedure for that program after you insert the CD into your computer.

To disable AutoPlay, press and hold the Shift key while inserting a removable disc.

See also the next subsection.

## Controlling the AutoPlay notice

Sometimes when you insert a removable disc, Windows may try to guess what action to take with the disc, or a dialog box may appear and prompt you to tell Windows what to do.

From the list, you can direct what Windows does with the disc.

To not do anything, choose the option labeled Take No Action.

Whether or not Windows displays the AutoPlay notice is up to you.
The window is controlled from the removable drive's Properties
dialog box:

1. Open the My Computer icon on the desktop.

2. Right-click the removable drive's icon.

   A pop-up menu appears.

3. Choose Properties from the pop-up menu.

4. Click the AutoPlay tab.

5. To disable AutoPlay, choose the item labeled Select an Action
   to Perform, and then choose the item labeled Take No Action.

6. Click OK.

   You can also close the My Computer window.

The removable drive's Properties dialog box can also be used to
preset what action to take or in what manner you would prefer that
Windows deal with removable disc. In Step 5 in the preceding
steps, simply choose the general disc type from the drop-down list
or select a program to take over when any disc is inserted.

## Types of shiny discs

There exists a variety of CDs and DVDs. Originally, there were just
CD-ROM and DVD-ROM. (Often, the "ROM" part isn't used when
describing the disc.) Beyond those two read-only formats are CDs
and DVDs that can be written to, by saving information similar to
other disk drives in your computer system.

To use recordable CDs and DVDs , your PC must be equipped with
the proper CD or DVD drive, one that can record information as
well as read it from the disc. The type of drive you have determines
which type of disc you can record to. Plus, you need special software that controls the recording process.

Here are the currently popular types of recordable CDs and DVDs:

**CD-R:** This type of CD can be written to, but only once. After the CD
is *burned,* it can be used in any computer and read just like any CD.
Data and music CDs can be created by using CD-Rs. Note that some
CD-Rs are specifically manufactured for music and others are made
for data. The label on the CD-R package tells you which is which.

**CD-RW:** This type of CD can be written to just like a CD-R. Unlike a
CD-R, however, this disc can be completely erased and used again,
if needed. These discs are slightly more expensive than regular
CD-Rs and can be played only on CD-RW-compatible CD players.

**DVD-R:** The most compatible format, DVD-R can be played on most computer DVD players as well as on video DVD players. If you want to make "home movie" DVDs, this is the format you want.

**DVD-RW:** This format is the same as DVD-R, though the discs can be completely erased and used again.

**DVD+R:** A write-once version of the DVD+RW format. This format is more efficient than the DVD-R format, though it's not widely supported.

**DVD+RW:** In this DVD-writing format, the disc can be erased and used over again. This format is very efficient, but it's not fully compatible with all DVD drives.

**DVD-RAM:** The oldest writeable DVD format is completely incompatible with all other DVD formats and is rarely used any more.

Some DVD discs allow recording on both sides of the disc. These double-sided discs sport a capacity of 9.4GB, which is simply double the 4.7GB you get on the single side of a DVD.

## Turning on recording

You must ensure that recording is enabled on a CD or DVD drive. For some reason, some PCs come with recording disabled. To quickly check, follow these steps:

1. Open the My Computer icon on the desktop.

2. Right-click the removable drive's icon.

3. Choose Properties from the pop-up menu.

4. Click the Recording tab.

   If there is no Recording tab, the drive is most likely a plain CD or DVD drive; you cannot use the drive to make your own CDs or DVDs .

5. Ensure that there is a check mark by the item labeled Enable CD Recording on This Drive.

6. Click the OK button.

   You can optionally close the My Computer window.

See also Part X for more information on creating your own CDs.

# Drive Icons

Windows assigns unique icons to different types of disk drives. These can be seen in the My Computer window, as well as in other locations in Windows where disk drives are referenced:

 The floppy drive icon is used only with Drive A, though other floppy drives that are added to the system share this icon.

 This is the hard drive icon.

 The CD/DVD drive icon is the same for both CD and DVD drives. But whenever you stick a CD or DVD disc into the drive, the icon changes. It's labeled either CD or DVD, or it may take on a new appearance based on the contents of the disc.

 The music CD icon replaces the standard CD or DVD icon whenever a musical CD is inserted into the drive.

 All removable drives, such as flash memory drives, share this icon.

 Zip disks appear with their own, unique icon — unless the Zip software isn't running, in which case the generic "removable drive" icon appears instead.

Some disk icons have special attachments underneath. The two most popular deal with networking:

 A shared drive on the network available to others on a computer network. (This addition may also appear beneath a folder icon.)

 The icon in the margin shows a network drive. When your computer accesses a disk drive or folder available on the network, that drive or folder's icon appears with pipes beneath it. That's your clue that the disk drive really lives elsewhere on the network.

# Drive Letters

Disk drives in your PC are assigned famous letters of the alphabet, starting with A and moving on from there. This is a historical thing with PCs, dating back to the first PC, which lacked a hard drive. That explains why the drive letter assignment isn't exactly logical.

✓ **Drive A:** Drive A is reserved for the PC's floppy drive, even if your PC doesn't have a floppy drive.

✓ **Drive B:** Drive B isn't used on modern PCs. Originally, it was assigned to the PC's second floppy drive.

✔ **Drive C:** Drive C is the first hard drive. This is the PC's main hard drive, the one on which the operating system (Windows) is found.

✔ **Drive D:** Drive letters D and up are assigned to any additional hard drives and then to removable drives inside the PC. They're assigned in sequence as the computer's software recognizes the drives when the PC first starts.

✔ **Drive Z:** The highest letter allowed for any disk drive on your PC is drive letter Z.

It's important to remember that not every PC uses the same letter for the same types of drives. Just because drive D is the CD-ROM on your computer doesn't mean that drive D is always the CD-ROM drive on every PC.

# Flash Memory Drives

The PC is designed to instantly recognize any flash memory drive attached to a USB port. Some drives may be plugged in directly, such as the USB jump drive. Other drives may require a card reader, such as a CompactFlash card reader, into which the memory card is plugged.

One big advantage to the flash memory drive is that you can use the drive to move information between computers. That was once the floppy disk's job, but flash memory drives hold far more information than floppy disks. They're also compact and portable and don't require batteries or other nuisances.

Another advantage: Your digital camera most likely stores images on a flash memory drive or media card. As long as your PC has a compatible card reader, you can easily transfer the images from your camera to the computer.

Several things may happen when a flash memory drive is plugged into the computer:

✔ A dialog box appears, asking what you want to do with the disk. See also "Controlling the AutoPlay notice."

✔ An icon for the disk appears in the My Computer window.

✔ A program may automatically run.

✔ The disk is assigned a drive letter.

Programs can access the disk and its files after Windows has successfully *mounted* the disk, or added it to your computer system.

Do not remove a flash memory drive while the computer is still using it!

See also Part II for information on removing, or unmounting, flash memory drives.

# The Floppy Drive

The former king of removable disk storage was the floppy drive and its floppy disk.

For years, the development of the floppy disk paralleled the development of the PC. Floppy disks grew from storing only 180KB of information on a single-sided 5¼-inch disk (that was really floppy), to storing 1.44MB of information on a double-sided 3½-inch disk. But there the floppy disk development stopped.

Computer memory capacity increased. Hard drive storage capacity increased. Combine that with the coming of the computer CD, and the floppy drive's future was doomed from the early 1990s. Even so, many PCs still come with floppy disks, mostly for compatibility. Sadly, the typical floppy disk still holds only a paltry 1.44MB of information — hardly enough.

The future of the floppy disk is certain: It's doomed. Already, PCs are being sold without those drives. If your computer has a floppy drive, you may never use it.

The PC's one and only floppy drive is labeled Drive A. This is consistent with all PCs.

The floppy drive consumes a standard PC floppy disk. The disk is composed of iron-oxide-coated Mylar, similar to the stuff that cassette and videotape is made of, but of a much higher quality, to store computer data.

The floppy disk is contained inside a hard-plastic, 3½-inch shell. The shell has a sliding door to protect the disk.

Don't touch the floppy disk itself, although you can freely handle the outer shell.

Floppy disks can be purchased at any computer or office supply store. Buy the disks labeled IBM PC-compatible. Avoid disks for the Macintosh or other computers.

To save time, buy floppy disks that are preformatted.

## Inserting a floppy disk

Floppy disks must be inserted into the floppy drive in order for them to be useful. Stick the disk into the drive with the label side up and the metal cover in first.

After you push the disk in almost all the way, the drive mechanism grabs the disk and quickly pulls it in the rest of the way. This makes a pleasing "thunk" sound.

## Ejecting a floppy disk

Don't eject any floppy disk you're still using. Be certain that all the files you've opened are saved and closed. Be certain that any open window displaying the floppy disk's contents is closed.

To eject the disk, push the ejection button by the floppy disk's hole. This pushes the disk out of the drive just a tiny bit. Pinch the disk with your fingers and remove it the rest of the way.

## Formatting floppies

Unlike with any other type of disk, a floppy disk must be *formatted* before you can use it. This formatting is merely a technical process that prepares the disk for use, for storing information.

Formatting can also be done to completely erase a disk and start over afresh. In this case, it's also referred to as reformatting.

Here's how you format or reformat a floppy disk:

*1.* Insert the floppy disk into Drive A.

   Any information already on the disk is erased by formatting. Do not format any disk you do not want to fully erase.

*2.* Open the My Computer icon on the desktop.

*3.* Select Drive A, the floppy drive.

*4.* Choose File⇨Format.

   There's no need to mess with any of the settings in the Format dialog box. If you're merely reformatting a disk, however, you can click the Quick Format option, which saves some time.

*5.* Click the Start button.

*6.* If a warning dialog box appears, click the OK button to continue with the format operation.

*7.* Wait and watch; this takes some time.

If the disk fails to format, you can try again: Start over with Step 2. Or, you can try formatting the disk on another PC. The tolerances of floppy drives varies from PC to PC. Or, you can just toss the floppy disk out.

**8.** Click OK to confirm that formatting is complete.

You can optionally remove the disk here, insert another floppy disk, and click the Start button to format the disk.

**9.** When you're done, click the Close button to dismiss the Format dialog box.

**10.** Use your floppy disk.

## Copying a file to Drive A

A floppy disk is used just like any other disk in your computer system. You merely choose that disk from a window or from the Address bar's drop-down list. Then, you can start using the files stored on a floppy disk.

To copy a file to Drive A, regard these steps:

**1.** Ensure that a formatted floppy disk is in Drive A.

**2.** Select the file or group of files.

**3.** Choose File⇨Send To⇨3½ Floppy (A:) from the menu.

To copy files from Drive A, follow these steps:

**1.** Insert the floppy disk into Drive A.

**2.** Open the My Computer icon on the desktop.

**3.** Open the floppy drive (A) icon.

**4.** Select the files to copy.

**5.** Choose Edit⇨Copy to Folder.

**6.** Use the Copy Items dialog box to locate a destination for the files you want to copy.

You can choose another disk drive from the list, or a specific folder on a disk drive.

**7.** Click the Copy button to copy the files from Drive A.

Remember to remove the floppy disk from Drive A when you're done with it.

See also Part VI, for more information on working with files.

## Floppy do's and don'ts

Don't save information directly to a floppy disk. Save to the hard drive first; use the floppy disk only for *copies* of information.

Don't download information from the Internet directly to a floppy disk. Someone somewhere offered this as a "tip" once, but it's not a tip. It's a gross mistake because the floppy disk cannot handle most downloads. Download to the hard drive, which is why your PC has a hard drive.

Remember to remove the floppy disk when you're done with it. If you forget, the PC may try to start itself from the floppy disk, which results in an error message. (Remove the disk in that case, and then press the Enter key to continue starting the PC.)

Don't try to eject or remove a floppy disk when the floppy drive's light is on. The light indicates that the computer is reading the disk. It's a bad thing to remove a floppy disk while the computer is reading from that disk.

Floppy disks come with labels. Use them! Peel and stick the label on the disk and give the disk a descriptive name.

Don't use a sticky note as a floppy disk's label. Those notes can peel off and get stuck inside the drive.

Don't insert a floppy disk into a Zip disc or CD-ROM drive. Likewise, don't try to wedge a floppy disk into one of the PC's cooling vents.

Don't remove a floppy disk from the drive until you're done with it. That means that any open window referring to the floppy disk is closed and that any files you've opened from the floppy disk are saved and closed.

Avoid getting a floppy disk wet.

Don't leave a floppy disk in direct sunlight because it will warp and damage the disk.

Don't leave the floppy disk around magnets, which erases the disk's contents. Magnets can be found in speakers, so don't leave a floppy disk on or near your PC's speakers.

Avoid the temptation to use a floppy disk as a drink coaster.

Floppy disks go bad over time. That's because the disk itself is being rubbed by the drive as information is written to and read from the disk. Therefore, don't keep any valuable information on the floppy disk only.

# Hard Disks and Drives

This is the skinny on the hard disk/hard drive puzzle: The *hard drive* is the physical unit. It's the whole enchilada. A hard disk lives inside the hard drive. So, unlike a floppy drive, where the floppy disk can be removed from the floppy drive, the hard disk inside the hard drive isn't going anywhere.

Technically, you should use the term hard drive to refer to the main source of long-term storage inside your PC: Drive C, Drive D, and so on.

Another term for a hard drive is a *fixed disk* because the disk cannot be removed. It's "fixed" inside the hard drive. (In this sense, fixed means immobile, not repaired.)

All PCs have at least one hard drive, which is called Drive C.

Your PC can have additional hard drives, given letters D and higher.

External hard drives can also be added to the system.

It's possible for one physical hard drive to be split up into separate or logical hard drives. For example, a 100GB hard drive can be *partitioned* into two 50GB hard drives. This partitioning is usually done at the factory or when the disk is first installed.

# Putting a Drive's Shortcut Icon on the Desktop

One way to make a disk drive handy is to put a shortcut to that drive on the desktop. Here are those all-important steps:

1. Open the My Computer icon on the desktop.

2. Click to select the drive icon you want to place on the desktop.

3. Choose Edit⇨Copy.

4. Close the My Computer window.

5. Right-click the desktop.

6. Choose Paste Shortcut from the pop-up menu.

The drive's icon now appears as a shortcut on the desktop for handy access.

You can rename the icon by using the standard file-renaming command (see also Part VII).

You can also put shortcuts to folders on the desktop (see also Part VII).

It's okay to delete a shortcut icon, even a shortcut icon for a disk drive. This doesn't erase the drive or remove the drive from your system; you can always access the drive from the My Computer window.

## Types of Drives

There are many things a PC can use that fall under the general term *drive* or *disk drive*. The bottom line is that these things are all media, or permanent storage.

Most PCs come with the three standard types of permanent storage, or disk drives:

- **Hard drive:** Primary storage. Pluses: Fast, cheap, high capacity. Minus: Not removable.

- **Floppy drive:** Secondary storage. Pluses: Widely used, removable. Minuses: Very low capacity, unreliable.

- **CD-ROM drive:** Massive storage and distribution of new software. Pluses: Removable, widely used, reliable. Minuses: Read-only, slow.

These types of disk drives or permanent storage are also popular:

- **DVD drive:** The super CD; stores almost seven times what a CD can hold. Pluses: Widely used, removable. Minuses: Read-only, slow.

- **Recordable CD/DVD drives (of various types):** An outstanding choice for removable, recordable media. Pluses: Recordable, removable. Minuses: Confusion over DVD recordable formats, some incompatibilities.

- **Flash memory:** Another handy form of removable storage. Pluses: Inexpensive, common, easy to use. Minuses: Relatively low capacity, slow.

- **Zip disc:** A great floppy disk replacement. Pluses: Easy to use, high-capacity compared to floppies, good support. Minuses: Not universally used, disks are expensive, slow.

There are even more forms of permanent storage. At one time or another, these were various disk drives you could have attached to a PC:

✔ **WORM drive:** The Write-Once Read Many removable drive was popular in the early 1990s, but never really gained wide use. It's really not necessary now that recordable CDs and DVDs are used.

✔ **MO drive:** The *m*agneto-optical drive was a removable disk format that recorded multiple megabytes on a single disk. As with the WORM drive, recordable CDs and DVDs have made this drive obsolete.

✔ **Bernoulli drive:** A high-capacity removable disk system of the early 1990s; it eventually evolved into the Zip disc system.

✔ **Tape backup or DAT drive:** These drives were once popular for PC backups, but are now found only in use on high-end servers.

✔ **Removable hard drive:** A temporary solution for folks who wanted removable information in high capacities; it was replaced by recordable CDs and DVDs, though various removable hard drive systems are still available and in use.

✔ **Super floppy drive:** A one-time solution for the obsolete floppy drive, the SuperDrive ate floppy disks as well as its own high-capacity disks.

✔ **Jaz drive:** The Zip disc's big brother is capable of holding gigabytes of information.

Some of these more esoteric drives may still be available; I believe Iomega (the Zip disc people) still makes the Jaz drive. Others were temporary solutions to problems long since solved in the technical arena.

# The Stuff You Create

The list of things a computer can do grows longer every year, as PCs become more powerful and people discover new and crazy things that they can do with computers. One of the things you do a lot on your PC is create stuff. Or, maybe you collect stuff, such as programs, videos, music, and other whatnot from the Internet.

On the computer, the stuff you create is stored in a compact unit called a file. A *file* is nothing more than a collection of stuff — data, information, text, music, and graphics, for example — stored in a compact unit. On your CD player, stuff comes on a CD. In a library, stuff is stored in books. On your PC, stuff is stored in files. And, you can do many things with files, mostly to keep them organized and keep yourself from going insane.

## In this part . . .

# *About a File*

The file itself is a collection of stuff on disk. The contents can be anything, thanks to the versatility of the computer. Even so, the contents are the most important part about the file, just as the contents of a container are more important than the container itself.

The file is merely a bunch of binary digits — raw computer information. In fact, the file really doesn't know what its contents are. Other things tell the operating system about what's in a file, but on a basic level, all files are merely digital information stored inside the computer.

Files are stored on disk. They are created in memory, but then that information is saved into the file "unit" on a disk drive.

On the PC, files are stored primarily on the hard drive.

Files can also be stored on removable disks, floppy disks, or flash drives and burned onto CD or DVD recordable discs.

Another term for the stuff inside a file is data. *Data* is just the fancy computer term for "stuff" or "information."

## Describing a file

As with other things that exist, there are various ways to describe a file. These ways are called file *attributes*. Here are just a few of the attributes used to describe a file stored on your computer, as well as to tell the operating system about the file's contents:

- **Filename:** The name used to identify the file. The name is given when the file is first saved to disk. Hopefully, the name is descriptive and not too long.

- **Filename extension:** The last part of the filename, in which a one- to-four-character code gives a hint about the file's contents or the type of file.

- **File type:** A term related to the filename extension. It gives a clue to the file's contents or the program that created it.

- **Icon:** In the Windows graphical environment, the tiny pictures given to files to represent their presence. The icon that appears depends on the file type, which the computer knows by reading in the filename extension.

- **File size:** The number of bytes, or characters, that the file occupies.

✔ **File creation date:** The date that the file was first created and saved to disk.

✔ **File modified date:** The date the file was last written to, changed, or modified.

✔ **Attributes:** Determines whether the file is hidden (invisible), is a system file, is compressed, has been backed up, is read-only, or has a number of other interesting effects or conditions.

Even more tidbits of information are available about a file, but those are too technical to bother with here.

## Common file icons

There are zillions of icons for the zillions of types of files that exist. Even so, certain files are common and identified by common icons. Here's a small sampling:

| *Icon* | *Extension* | *File Type* |
|---|---|---|
| | BMP | Windows Paint graphics; bitmap image |
| | DOC | Word processing document; Microsoft Word document |
| | XLS | Microsoft Excel worksheet document |
| | EXE or COM | Generic program file, though most program files have their own, unique icons |
| | (Varies) | Generic file, no specific type |
| | GIF | GIF graphics image |
| | HTM or HTML | Web page or HTML document |
| | JPG or JPEG | JPEG graphics image |
| | WMP | Sound and video, for example |
| | PDF | Adobe Acrobat Reader document |
| | TXT or TEXT | Plain text |

The Generic icon is assigned to files that don't have a specific type. After all, every file must have an icon.

## Viewing file details in Windows Explorer

The best way to get more information about a file is to view it, to locate that file by using the Windows Explorer program (see also Part VII) and look at the file.

Immediately, the file's icon tells you a bit about the file, especially if you can recognize the file's icon. Otherwise, to see more information, you have two options.

First, use the Details information panel on the left side of the window. This area displays brief file details on any individual icon selected.

Second, you can choose to view the folder window in Details view. Choose View⇨Details from the menu. This action changes the window's display to show files in a list, with columns describing further information.

The columns display various attributes about the file: name, size, file type, date, and other optional information.

You can adjust the columns, and the window's display, in many ways:

✔ The list of files can be sorted based on any column; simply click the column header. Click the same column header again to sort the list in reverse order.

✔ The column used to sort the list has a triangle by its name. The triangle points up or down, depending on how the column is sorted (in ascending or descending order).

✔ Columns can easily be rearranged. Use the mouse to drag a column heading left or right. This action changes the column order. For example, to put the Type column before the Size column, drag the Type column heading to the left of the Size column.

✔ Columns can be resized by dragging the right edge of the column's heading left or right. Double-clicking the right edge resizes the column's width to match the widest item in that column.

You can add or remove columns from the Windows Explorer windows, in Details view: Right-click the mouse on any header. This action displays a menu full of optional headers. Selected headers have check marks by them.

If you choose the More option from the header menu, a Choose Details dialog box appears. That's a more manageable place to choose which details to hide or show in Windows Explorer, in Details view.

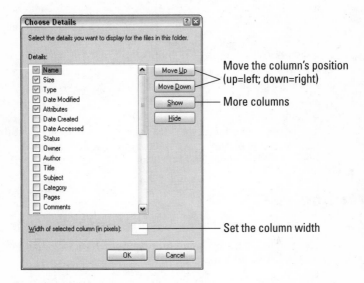

Move the column's position (up=left; down=right)

More columns

Set the column width

Not every potential column applies to every file. Most columns describe attributes of music files.

## A file's Properties dialog box

Information about any file can be discovered by viewing the file's Properties dialog box. To see it, right-click the file's icon and choose the Properties command from the pop-up menu.

A file's Properties dialog box has two or more tabs. The first one is the General tab, which offers lots of descriptive information about the file.

The other tabs offer further descriptive information about the file or, depending on the type of file, can be used to modify settings or control certain specifics of the file.

# Creating Files

Files come into existence in one of three ways:

✔ You use software on your computer to create something and save that stuff to disk as a file.

✔ You copy a file from another computer, either over a network or from a removable disk.

✔ You download a file from the Internet.

No matter what, all files are created on some computer somewhere. The file starts out as something in memory, which is then saved to a disk somewhere as a file. From there, it can go anywhere, by moving to other computers across a network or the Internet or being transferred between two computers on a removable disk.

The operating system, as well as other programs, creates files as needed. These are typically temporary files. The temporary files are deleted when they're no longer needed.

# Finding Lost Files

Files get lost all the time. They're misplaced or they're copied or saved into the wrong folder, or you may just forget whatever crazy names you assigned to them. Lost files happen to beginners and experienced users and organized and unorganized users alike.

The following sections are specific to Windows XP. (The methods for finding files in earlier versions of Windows are radically different.)

## Summoning the Search Companion

In Windows XP, it's the Search Companion that helps you locate long-lost files. The Search Companion is a special task pane on the left side of the Windows Explorer window. It can be summoned in several ways:

✔ Click the Search button.

✔ Choose View⇨Explorer Bar⇨Search.

✔ Press Ctrl+E.

✔ Press the F3 key.

✔ Choose the Search command from the Start button's menu.

This section assumes that you know how to summon the Search Companion window.

Yes, you can mix and match options. The more information you can provide about a missing file, the easier (and faster) Windows finds it.

When the Search Companion finds files, they're listed in the window, similar to the way Windows Explorer displays files in Details view. After the files are listed, you can click to select a file and then manipulate it however you want. To open the folder window where the file lives, click to select the file and choose File⇨Open Containing Folder.

## Finding a file when you know its name

Summon the Search Companion and follow these steps:

1. Choose the item labeled All Files and Folders.

2. Type the name into the text box labeled All or Part of the File Name.

   As it says, you can type part of the name, all of the name, or even something remotely close to the name.

3. Choose where to look for the file from the drop-down list labeled Look In.

   You can limit the search to the My Documents folder (and its subfolders) or search other disk drives or other parts of Drive C. The more places you search, the longer the search takes.

4. Click the Search button.

## Finding a file when you just created it recently

Beckon forth the Search Companion and pursue these steps:

1. Choose the item labeled All Files and Folders.

2. Click the downward-pointing arrow by the item labeled When Was It Modified?

3. Select a duration, either by choosing from the list or entering specific dates where prompted.

4. Click the Search button.

## Finding a file when you know what type of file it is

Muster the Search Companion and heed these steps:

1. Choose the item labeled All Files and Folders.

2. Click the downward-pointing arrow by the item labeled More Advanced Options.

3. Choose the application that created the file, or the file type, from the drop-down list labeled Type of File.

4. Click the Search button.

## Finding a file when you know that it contains a specific word

Conjure up the Search Companion and incant these steps:

1. Choose the item labeled All Files and Folders.

2. Type the text to find into the box labeled A Word or Phrase in the File.

3. Because this search tends to be the most time-consuming type that Windows does, any further information you can specify is useful.

4. Click the Search button.

# Managing Files

To help keep your files organized, Windows supplies you with a host of file-manipulating tools. You can copy, move, delete, and undelete files.

## Copying files

When you copy a file, you create a duplicate of that file — an exact copy — in another folder or on another disk drive. In Windows, there are many ways to do this. Here are the most popular ways to copy a single file or group of select files:

**Copy and paste.** Select the files to be copied and choose Edit⇨ Copy from the menu. Open the folder or disk drive window where you want to place the copies. In that window, choose the Edit⇨ Paste command.

**Copy to folder.** Select the files to be copied and choose Edit⇨Copy to Folder from the menu. Use the Copy to Folder window to locate the disk drive or folder for the file copies. Click to select that folder, and then click the Copy button.

**Dragging to copy.** You need to have two windows open and visible on the desktop: the folder containing the original file and the folder to which you want to copy the file. Press and hold the Ctrl key on the keyboard, and then use the mouse to drag the file from one window to the other. (Pressing the Ctrl key ensures that the file is copied and not moved.)

You can use these techniques to copy a file to another folder on the same hard drive or to another disk drive.

## Duplicating files

A file *duplicate* is merely a copy of a file made in the same folder:

1. Select the file to be duplicated.

2. Choose Edit⇨Copy.

3. Choose Edit⇨Paste.

The file is duplicated in the same folder, but with the text "Copy of" prefixed to its name. The duplicate has the same contents, is the same size, and is the same type of file as the original.

See also "Making file shortcuts."

## Moving files

When you move a file, you create a duplicate of that file — just like a file copy, but the original is then destroyed. Windows has many commands for moving a file or group of selected files, and these are the most popular:

**Cut and Paste.** Select the files you want to move and then, from the menu, choose Edit⇨Cut. The file isn't deleted at this point, but is ready to be moved. Next, open the folder or disk drive window where you want to move the files. Choose the Edit⇨Paste command from that window's menu. The file is then moved; the original is deleted.

**Move to Folder.** Select the files you want to move and choose Edit⇨Copy to Folder. In the Move to Folder window, choose the disk drive or folder where you want to move the file. Select that folder, and then click the Move button.

**Dragging to Move.** Open two folder windows on the desktop. The first window contains the file to be moved. The second window is the folder or disk drive to where you want the file moved. Use the mouse to drag the file from the first window to the second. If you're dragging the file to another disk drive, press and hold the Shift key while you drag the mouse; that action ensures that the file is moved and not copied.

## Making file shortcuts

A *shortcut* is the same thing as a file copy, but without all the bulk of making a file copy. In a way, the shortcut is simply a placeholder icon. Internally, the icon references the original file so that when you open the shortcut, the original file opens instead.

Creating a shortcut works just like copying a file with the Edit⇨ Copy command. The difference is that you make the shortcut by using Edit⇨Paste Shortcut.

 A shortcut icon is flagged by a tiny arrow in its lower-left corner.

You can move, copy, rename, or delete a shortcut icon. Doing so doesn't affect the original file.

Moving, renaming, or deleting the original icon doesn't update the shortcut icon. In this case, the shortcut may get "lost." When you try to open the shortcut, Windows attempts to locate the original for you.

It's important to remember that a file shortcut works only on your computer. You cannot e-mail a file shortcut to another computer and have it work. If you need to send a copy of a file to another computer, send a copy of the original; don't create a shortcut.

## Deleting files

To delete a file, click to select the file's icon and choose File➪Delete from the menu. You can also use the Delete key on the computer's keyboard as a shortcut.

A warning may appear when you delete a file, to confirm that you really want to delete it.

Deleting a file sends it to the Recycle Bin, where it sits and awaits undeleting. But, note that after a while, all files are purged from the Recycle Bin; therefore, don't be casual when you're deleting files you may want to recover later.

## Permanently deleting files

If you want to delete a file permanently, select the file's icon and press Shift+Delete on the keyboard. This action doesn't transfer the file to the Recycle Bin, but instead utterly removes it from your computer system. This type of deleted file cannot be recovered by using Windows.

## Undeleting files

To recover a file you deleted, you must rescue it from the Recycle Bin:

1.  Open the Recycle Bin icon on the desktop.

2.  Choose View➪Details.

    This step arranges the items in the bin by columns, which makes it easier to sort and sift through them for what you want.

3.  If you know the filename, click the Name column heading to sort the deleted files by name; if you know the date the file was deleted, click the Date Deleted column head.

4.  Click to select the files you want to undelete.

5.  Choose File➪Restore from the menu.

    The file is returned to the folder from which it was deleted.

6.  Close the Recycle Bin window.

Note that you cannot preview or open files stored in the Recycle Bin.

If you want to put the file in another folder, follow the preceding steps to restore it to its original folder, and then move it to the folder you want after it has been restored.

# Naming and Renaming Files

All files in the computer need to be given a name. Here are the official rules:

- Filenames can contain letters, numbers, spaces, and most of the symbols you find on the computer keyboard.

- A filename must be at least one character long.

- Filenames can be up to 254 characters long.

- Filenames cannot contain these specific characters:

    "   *   /   :   ?   \   |   <   >

- Contrary to popular myth, you can start a filename with a number or punctuation symbol.

- Two files in the same folder cannot have the same name.

Short, descriptive filenames are best. (As filenames get longer, it's more difficult to see their full names displayed in a folder window.)

Windows isn't case sensitive when it comes to filenames. You can use upper- or lowercase letters, but internally Windows sees all files as uppercase. Note that other operating systems, as well as many Web page addresses, are case sensitive.

Although spaces are allowed in a filename, many users opt to use underlines instead. For example:

```
Special_Finance_Report
```

## The filename extension

A very special and important part of a filename is its extension. This is the last part of a filename, which begins with a period and is followed by up to four characters. Those characters are used in Windows to identify the file type.

See also "Common file icons" for a sample list of filename extensions.

## Renaming a file

You can change the name of a file by using the Rename command:

1. Select the file or icon you want to rename.

2. Choose File⇨Rename from the menu.

3. Type the file's new name.

4. Press the Enter key to lock in the new name.

If Windows doesn't let you rename a file, you're probably using a forbidden character in the name or trying to use the name of a file already in the folder. Try again.

When you rename a file, don't rename its extension. Doing so changes the file type, which isn't correct because renaming a file doesn't change the file's contents. (The extension may or may not be visible in the folder window; see also Part VII.)

You can use the standard Windows editing keys when you rename a file. You can move the cursor left or right, select text, delete or insert text, and do just about anything else that you can do with regular text when you rename a file.

## Filename wildcards

Windows uses two characters, * and ?, as wildcards when specifying filenames. These wildcards can be used when you're searching for files, to help narrow or expand the search when you may not know all of a file's name.

The ? character is used to represent any single character in a filename.

The * character is used to represent a group of characters in a filename. Or, the * can be used by itself to represent all files.

Two other wildcards exist: . (dot) and .. (dot-dot). The single dot represents the current folder, or all the files in the current folder. The double dot represents the parent folder. See also Part VII for more information on folders and parent folders.

# Opening Files

To work on a file — a document, graphical image, music file, or anything you have created or collected — you need to open that file on disk. There are several ways to do this:

✔ Locate the file's icon somewhere in a folder window. Double-click the icon to open it, which also starts the program that created the file.

✔ Locate a shortcut icon to the file. Opening the shortcut opens the original file itself.

✔ **Open the application that you will use to work on the file.** Choose File⇨Open from the menu and use the Open dialog box to locate the file on whatever disk drive or whatever folder the file was last saved. The keyboard shortcut for File⇨Open is Ctrl+O.

✔ From the Start button's menu, locate the My Recent Documents submenu and choose the file from there (only recently opened files appear on the list).

Opening a file opens the application that created that file — unless another application has priority. For example, opening a Paint document (graphical image) in Windows XP displays the image in the Windows Picture and Fax Viewer program, not Paint.

When Windows cannot locate a program to open a file, it displays an Open With dialog box. The best thing to do in this case is click the Cancel button. Windows cannot open the program, or the application that created the program isn't available.

To open a file in a specific program, right-click the file's icon and choose Open With from the pop-up menu. Then, you can select a specific program from the Open With submenu, and the file is opened by that program.

## Pathnames

A pathname is like an address. This is easy to understand if you use the Internet; a *pathname* is similar to a Web page address except that the pathname refers to locations on your computer and not on the Internet.

A pathname has several parts, some of which are optional:

✔ **Drive letter.** The drive letter is always followed by a colon.

✔ **Folders.** Starting with the root folder, represented by a single backslash, the pathname lists each folder up to the specified location. Each folder name is separated by a backslash character.

✔ **Filename.** After the last backslash comes an optional filename, complete with extension.

A *full pathname* contains all these elements. It starts with a drive letter and colon, and then it lists folders down to a filename. For example:

```
C:\Windows\System32\Restore\rstrui.exe
```

The full pathname starts with a drive letter, colon, and folders separated by backslashes, and then ends with a filename. To get to that file, you follow the path: Change to Drive C; change to the Windows folder, the System32 folder, and then the Restore folder; and then you can locate the RSTRUI.EXE program.

A full pathname can be used to run or open any program or file. The full pathname is merely a specific name telling the computer where to find a file.

A partial pathname may be used to give the location for some files. For example, you may tell a co-worker to find the graphics files on this path on your computer:

`My Documents\Projects\2005\Summer\2341\Images`

Using the path, you know to start in the My Documents folder and then open the following folders: Projects, 2005, Summer, 2341, and, finally, the Images folder.

The drive letter can be replaced by the name of another computer on the network. In this case, the pathname becomes a *network path*. For example:

`\\MING\Shared\current`

The two backslashes at the start of the path identify a network pathname. The network computer is named MING. The folder being shared by MING is named Shared. The subfolder named `current` is the location the network pathname refers to.

You often see pathnames specified on the Windows Explorer Address bar.

# *Saving Files*

Files are created by saving your stuff to disk. You work in a program. You make something. To keep it, you save it to disk.

Saving is simple: The computer does all the hard work. But the idea is important. You must save your stuff to disk so that you can have it later, just to keep, to modify, to print, or to do whatever you will. But, to do all that stuff, you have to save your stuff in the first place.

## Saving for the first time

Saving is a very common task, so it has a universal command: File⇨Save. From the keyboard, the shortcut is Ctrl+S. This is consistent for just about every program in Windows.

When you save something for the first time, a special Save As dialog box appears. It allows you to do up to four things:

✔ Assign a descriptive name to the file.

✔ Choose a location for the file.

✔ Create a new folder for the file (if necessary).

✔ Save the file as a special type (if necessary).

You don't have to type the filename extension when you're saving a file. The application automatically adds the proper extension for the type of file being saved.

## Saving after the first time

After the file is saved for the first time, it's associated with the file-name and location you specified in the Save As dialog box. To save the file again, which updates the file already on disk, you choose File⇨Save or use the Ctrl+S keyboard shortcut.

Saving a file after the first time is easy. By using the Save command, you simply update the existing file on disk with any updates you have made to the document or image you're working on.

Save often.

## Closing a document

The last thing you do with a document is close it. When you're done working on the document, or when you're done with the program, you can choose File⇨Close from the menu. If the document needs to be saved, you're asked to save it one last time. Then, the document is closed, safely saved on disk.

The keyboard shortcut for the Close command is Ctrl+W. This is common to most, but not all, programs.

If you just plan on quitting a program (you're done for the day), you can use the File⇨Exit command to both close the document (saving it to disk) and quit the program. The keyboard shortcut for closing a program is Alt+F.

# Selecting Icons

To work with more than one file at a time, you must select multiple files. These selected files can then be manipulated as a group, which saves time over repeatedly issuing commands on single files.

File commands in a folder affect all selected files.

Files can be selected in only one folder at a time. If you need to work with files in multiple folders, you must do so one folder window at a time.

You can do anything to a group of files that you can do to a single file — delete, copy, or move, for example. An exception is renaming a group of files. In that case, the group is given the same name, followed by a sequential number.

This section discusses the many techniques for selecting a group of files.

## Selecting a single icon

To select a single icon, click it with the mouse. The icon is then highlighted, indicating that it has been selected for action.

## Selecting all icons in a window

To select all the icons in a folder window, choose Edit⇨Select All from the menu. The keyboard shortcut is Ctrl+A.

## Selecting two or more individual icons

To select individual icons, it's best to use the Ctrl+click technique:

*1.* Press and hold the Ctrl key on the keyboard.

Either Ctrl (control) key works.

*2.* Click each icon that you want selected.

Each icon you click becomes selected, as long as you keep the Ctrl key down while clicking with the mouse.

Note that an icon stays selected even if you need to scroll around the window to search for new icons.

If you click the mouse (no Ctrl key) anywhere in the window, all selected files become deselected and you have to start over again.

## Lassoing a group of icons

To select a group of icons, drag the mouse over them. This is best done in Icon view: Choose View⇨Icons from the menu. Then, point the mouse above and to the left of the icons to be selected. Drag the mouse down and to the right to "lasso" them, or select a chunk of them at once.

## Selecting all but one icon

There are two quick ways to select all but one icon in a window.

The first method is to choose Edit⇨Select All to select all icons on the menu. Then, press and hold the Ctrl key on the keyboard and click the mouse on the sole icon you want unselected. Release the Ctrl key.

The second method is to select the one icon you *do not* want to select. Then, choose Edit⇨Invert Selection from the menu.

## Selecting all but a few icons

Start by selecting all the icons you don't want selected. Use Ctrl+click to pick those out. Then, choose Edit⇨Invert selection to select every other icon in the window.

## Selecting icons in a range

To choose icons in a range, you first need to create the range. Choose View⇨List from the menu to display the icons in a list. Then, you can choose View⇨Arrange Icons By and choose a method to list the icons from the submenu: by date, size, name, or type, for example.

Click the mouse to select the first icon in the range. Then, press and hold the Shift key and click the last icon in the range. This action selects all icons between the first click and the Shift+click.

## Selecting two ranges of icons

To select multiple ranges of icons, follow the instructions in the preceding subsection. To select the second range, press and hold the Ctrl key. Keep the Ctrl key down and click the first icon in the range. Release the Ctrl key. Press and hold Ctrl+Shift and click the last icon in the second range. Release Ctrl+Shift.

## Deselecting an icon from a group

Pressing and holding the Ctrl key while you click a selected icon unselects that icon. Release the Ctrl key when you're done deselecting.

# Organizing Your Stuff

As you use your computer, you collect and create stuff. Windows provides you with a few handy tools to help keep that stuff organized. Sadly, there are no suggestions or even tight rules for using those tools. Organization, it seems, is up to you.

On the whole, organization is a good thing. The more organized you keep your stuff, the better you can find it when you need it. That's the important part. Being organized makes your computer experience all the better. And, who wouldn't be thankful for that?

## In this part . . .

# About Folders

*Folders* are containers for files — just like in the real world.

In a computer, a folder can hold a huge, virtually unlimited, number of files. Of course, you don't want to pack zillions of files into a single folder. That would defeat the purpose. Instead, folders are used to keep like files together.

 A folder in Windows is flagged with a folder icon.

Opening the folder icon displays a window. The window lists the contents of, or files that live inside, the folder.

Folders can also contain other folders — folders within folders — just to keep things organized.

# About Windows Explorer

Windows uses a program named Windows Explorer to display the contents of folders and to list files (icons) in a window. It's a Windows Explorer window you see whenever you open a folder.

To start Windows Explorer, you simply find a folder and open it.

To manually start Windows Explorer, from the Start button's menu, choose All Programs➪Accessories➪Windows Explorer.

The keyboard shortcut for Windows Explorer is Win+E. If your computer keyboard lacks a Windows key, there is no keyboard shortcut.

## The left side of the window thing

In Windows XP, the left side of a Windows Explorer window shows three different things:

- ✔ The tree structure
- ✔ The Search Companion
- ✔ Various task panes

One of these is always showing; unlike previous versions of Windows, the dang thing will not go away.

 To switch to the tree structure, click the Folders button or choose View➪Explorer Bar➪Folders from the menu.

 To switch to the Search Companion, click the Search button or choose View➪Explorer Bar➪Search. The keyboard shortcut is Ctrl+E.

To see the task panes, click the X in the upper-right corner of the Folders or Search Companion thing.

## The tree structure

The *tree structure* lists the contents of your computer, beginning with the desktop and then going "down" from there. The purpose of the tree structure is to help you navigate through disk drives and the folders on those drives to help find the location you want. It's a shortcut.

An item in the tree structure has a plus or minus button by it if that item contains more information, such as a folder containing a sub-folder.

Clicking the plus button opens a folder to reveal its contents.

Clicking the minus button closes a folder.

You can also use the keyboard to navigate through the tree structure:

| Key | Action |
|-----|--------|
| Up | Move up |
| Down | Move down |
| Left | Move left or open a closed branch |
| Right | Move right or close an open branch |
| + | Open a branch (without moving) |
| - | Close a branch (without moving) |
| * | Open all branches |

## The Search Companion

The Search Companion is used to find wayward files. This subject is covered in detail in Part VI.

## The task pane

The task pane shows several areas of interest with shortcuts to common commands, links to other places, and detailed information about whatever is selected in the Windows Explorer window.

**File and Folder Tasks.** This pane lists common commands or actions to take, depending on what is selected in the Windows Explorer window.

**Other Places.** This pane lists other locations in Windows related to whatever item is selected.

**Details.** This pane shows information about the selected files — even a preview if a graphics file is selected.

Each of the panes can be open or shut by clicking the chevrons in their upper-right corners.

## The Address bar

The *Address bar* is an optional toolbar you can use to help increase the power of the Windows Explorer window. The *Address bar* displays the name of the current folder and the path to the current folder, or it can be used to enter a Web page address. And, if you know a pathname to a folder, you can type it on the Address bar, though that's a rather geeky thing to do.

To view the Address bar, choose View⇨Toolbars⇨Address Bar from the menu.

To see full pathnames displayed on the Address bar, obey these steps:

*1.* In Windows Explorer, choose Tools⇨Folder Options.

*2.* Click the View tab.

*3.* Put a check mark by the item labeled Display the Full Path in the Address Bar.

*4.* Click OK.

# Compressed (ZIP) Folders

A special type of folder in Windows is the *compressed* folder, also known as a ZIP file. This folder holds other files (and folders), just like any other folder in Windows. But the files inside it are compressed and take up less disk space.

Compressed folders aren't really used like regular folders for storing files. Instead, they work like shipping containers: You put into a compressed folder any stuff that you want to store or perhaps ship via e-mail elsewhere. The compressed folder keeps the various files together, plus it takes up less space, which makes the file-sending task take less time.

In Windows XP, compressed folders have their own, special zipper icon.

Note that the contents of compressed folders aren't usually searched when Windows performs a file search.

## Making a compressed folder

To create a compressed folder, choose File⇨New⇨Compressed (zipped) Folder. The new folder appears with the name New Compressed (zipped) Folder.zip.

Yes, you can rename the compressed folder, just as you would any other file or folder.

You can also create a compressed folder by first selecting one or more files in a window. To place those selected files into a compressed folder, choose File⇨Send To⇨Compressed (zipped) Folder. The files are packed into the compressed folder and given the name of the first file selected (but with the ZIP file extension).

## Adding files to a compressed folder

Adding files to a compressed folder works just like adding files to any other folder: You can drag and drop, open the window, and copy and paste.

You cannot, however use the Move This File or Copy This File command. Remember that compressed folders aren't real folders, and, therefore, you cannot access them from a tree structure.

## Extracting files

Most files cannot be accessed inside a compressed folder. Although you can view the file's icon, you cannot open the file. That's because it's compressed and needs to be decompressed before it can be useful.

To *extract,* or decompress, a file, open the compressed folder and select the file or group of files. Then, you can choose either Copy This File or Move This File from the File and Folder Tasks pane on the left side of the window.

To quickly extract all files from a compressed folder, choose File⇨ Extract All. The files are extracted completely and placed into a folder that's given the same name as the compressed folder — but it's a real folder with real files.

## Applying a password

Unlike with other types of files in Windows, you can apply a password to your compressed folders. To do so, open the compressed folder window and choose File⇨Add a Password from the menu.

Note that you cannot open the compressed folder again without that password. If you lose the password, the contents of the compressed folder are gone forever.

# Directories

The old, original term for a file folder was *directory*.

*Folder* is simply a newer term for *directory*.

A subfolder is the same thing as a subdirectory.

The root folder can also be called the root directory.

Although Microsoft shuns the term *directory,* occasionally you still see it used in documentation and bandied about by old-timers who refuse to change with the times.

# Folder Options

 The way folders look and behave in Windows is controlled via the Folder Options icon in the Control Panel. Opening that icon displays the Folder Options dialog box, which you can also display by choosing Tools⇨Folder Options from any Windows Explorer window.

Two tabs in the Folder Options dialog box control how a folder behaves: General and View.

On the General tab, you can control how folder windows work.

To show or hide the task pane in a folder window, select an option in the Tasks area. When you select Use Windows Classic Folders, for example, the task pane no longer shows up.

To open one window for every folder, use the Browse folders area. There, you can choose whether opening a new folder also opens a window or whether things stay in the same window.

Finally, the Click Item area lets you set whether one click or two does the job of opening things.

On the View tab, you can control various details about what shows up and what doesn't show up in a folder window.

One item worth noting is the display of *hidden* files. If you want hidden files to appear in a window, put a check mark by the item labeled Show Hidden Files and Folders. The folders appear as faded, ghost icons, but they show up nonetheless.

You can also elect to show all filename extensions, by removing the check mark by the item labeled Hide Extensions to Known File Types.

## Choosing a folder template

If you know that a specific folder will be used to hold a specific type of file — music, graphics, text — you can customize that folder with a template, which makes Windows really shine and offers you the best way to view certain types of files.

To modify a folder with a template, follow these steps:

1. Locate the folder, but don't open its window; just select the folder icon.

2. Choose File⇨Properties.

3. Click the Customize tab.

4. Select a template from the drop-down list.

   You can find different templates for pictures, music, and videos.

5. Click the OK button.

## Adding an image to a folder

To put a picture on a folder icon, supposedly to remind you of the folder's contents, follow these steps:

1. Right-click the folder you want to modify.

2. Choose Properties from the pop-up menu.

3. In the folder's Properties dialog box, click the Customize tab.

4. Click the Choose Pictures button.

5. Use the Browse dialog box to locate a suitable graphical image for the folder's face.

6. Click the Open button when you have found and selected an image.

7. Click the OK button.

Note that you can click the Restore Default button to remove the picture, in case you tire of it later.

Also note that the picture shows up only in Thumbnails view.

## Changing a folder icon

Rather than put a silly thumbnail picture on a folder, you can change the folder's icon to anything you please — or to any icon supplied with Windows. Here's how:

1. Right-click the folder you want to change.

2. From the pop-up menu, choose File⇨Properties.

3. Click the Customize tab.

4. Click the Change Icon button.

5. Browse in the Change Icon dialog box for a new icon.

   You can also use the Browse button there to locate another icon file on the hard drive, or an icon file you may have created yourself by using some graphics program.

6. Click OK when you have found a better icon.

7. Click the OK button.

The new icon shows up in all window views — except Thumbnail!

# Managing Folders

Folders can be tossed about, battered, and bruised, just like any file. Yet, it's important to remember that a folder isn't just a file; it's a location for other files. So, when you mess with a folder, you also mess with the folder's contents. Beware!

## Making a new folder

Open the folder window where you want to create the new folder. For example, to create a new folder in the My Documents folder, open the My Documents window.

Choose File⇨New⇨Folder from the menu. The new folder appears in the window, given the name New Folder. The name is selected, so you can immediately type a new name for the folder, something short and descriptive.

See also Part VI for file-naming rules, which also apply to folders (though folders don't normally have filename extensions).

## Removing a folder

To remove a folder, click to select it. Then, press the Delete key on your keyboard or choose File⇨Delete from the menu.

Deleting a folder removes all the folder's contents — files and sub-folders. Don't use this command casually. Never delete any folder you did not create yourself, such as any of the Windows folders or folders for programs.

You can recover a deleted folder from the Recycle Bin. See also Part VI for information on recovering a deleted file; the same directions can be used to restore a deleted folder.

To permanently delete a folder, press Shift+Delete on the keyboard.

## Renaming a folder

Folders can be renamed just like files: Click to select the folder and choose File⇨Rename from the menu. The keyboard shortcut is the F2 key.

See also Part VI for information on renaming files, all of which applies to folders as well.

Folders don't need filename extensions. Even if you apply an extension to a folder, it doesn't change the folder to a specific file type.

## Copying or moving a folder

To copy or move a folder, click to select it. Then, choose Edit⇨ Copy from the menu to duplicate the folder or Edit⇨Cut to move it. Open the destination folder window — the place where you want the folder copied or moved. Then, choose Edit⇨Paste from the menu.

To create a shortcut to the folder, choose Edit⇨Paste Shortcut. See also Part VI.

Note that moving folders tends to confuse programs that try to remember where your files are located. Don't move folders that contain programs because this action may render the programs unusable.

# *My Downloads Folder*

I recommend, as a tip, that you create a special folder for the files you download from the Internet. This includes programs and compressed folders — all that stuff should find its own, special place. I suggest the My Downloads folder:

*1.* Open the My Computer folder.

*2.* Choose File⇨New⇨Folder.

*3.* Press the F2 key to rename the new folder.

*4.* For the new name, type **My Downloads**.

Or, you can type **Downloads**, though the *My* prefix seems to be popular in Windows.

*5.* Press the Enter key to lock in the new name.

Now you can use the My Downloads folder whenever you're prompted to save a file when you're using Internet Explorer.

From the My Downloads folder, you can run installation programs or extract files from compressed folders.

I recommend keeping the original files in your My Documents folder, even after you have installed programs. That way, you can keep a spare copy, in case you want to reinstall the program later.

# The "My" Folders

Windows helps you along by doing a bit of folder organization for you. In this case, it creates what I call the *My* series of folders. Other programs may create other folders, but there are three key My Folders:

- My Documents
- My Pictures
- My Music

The *My Documents* folder is the home folder for all the stuff you create or collect. My Documents is where you should start creating other folders as the base for organizing your stuff.

The *My Pictures* folder is a home base for your graphics and picture files. It's a subfolder of the My Documents folder.

The *My Music* folder is a home base for all the music files on your computer. This folder is used by Windows Media Player, but you can put your own files there as well.

Feel free *not* to use the My Pictures or My Music folders. You can create your own folders and organize your stuff however you see fit. But don't bother deleting those folders. Windows own programs assume that the folders exist — and may even re-create them if needed.

# The Root Folder

There has to be a name for the main folder on a hard drive, and that name is *root*. The root folder is considered the first folder, or occasionally the only folder, on a disk. It's called the root because all other folders on that drive branch out from that folder, like the root of a tree.

The root folder is specified by a single backslash character, \.

Don't save any files directly in the root folder. Instead, create other folders in which you can place your files. If you use the root, the disk quickly becomes too crowded and confusing. Also, Windows places restrictions on files that are allowed to be in the root folder of Drive C.

An exception to the no-files-in-the-root-folder rule is for floppy disks. For those disks, as well as Zip disks and most other removable media, it's okay to put files in the root. But, for long-term storage, use folders instead.

# Subfolders

A *subfolder* is merely one folder inside another folder. So, when you create a folder named My Downloads inside the My Documents folder, the My Downloads folder is said to be a subfolder of the My Documents folder.

The opposite of a subfolder is a parent folder. Using the preceding example, the My Documents folder would be the parent folder of the My Downloads folder.

The root folder has no parent folder.

# Printing

Though a printer is considered an important part of the basic computer system, it's really more like a separate, customized computer all its own — complete with its own set of puzzlements and problems. You can put in effort all day long, and even save your stuff for good, but until it's printed, your efforts remain ambiguously digital. Only with that final printing duty can you really share your work with others. The proof is in the printing.

## In this part . . .

# Adding a Printer

As with most computer hardware, adding a printer to your computer system involves both hardware and software steps.

## Setting up a printer

Place the printer relatively close to your computer — within arm's reach so that you can pull out any paper or easily add paper.

Despite the printer's small size, remember that it may need extra space in front or behind to make room for paper trays that pop out or slide open.

Don't place the printer in direct sunlight. That may heat the printer up and make it woefully unhappy.

Printers don't come with cables! You must buy a cable separately. See also Part I.

See also "Adding paper to the printer" and "Ink and Toner."

## Attaching the printer hardware

Printers plug into the wall, which is how they get their power. Furthermore, the printer must be connected to the computer via a printer cable. The printer cable attaches to both the printer and the computer.

There are two types of printer cables:

- ✔ The traditional printer cable
- ✔ The USB cable

Both types of cable have two unique ends, so you cannot plug the cable in backward.

If you attach the printer by using the traditional printer cable, ensure that both the printer and computer are off. You can keep either the printer or computer on when using a USB cable.

See also "Turning the Printer On and Off."

## Printer software setup

See your printer's setup manual for specific instructions that may be necessary to set up your printer's software. For example, the instructions may direct you to install special software before turning on the printer for the first time.

Some USB printers may install themselves automatically when they're first connected and turned on.

To confirm that a printer is installed, look for an icon representing that printer in the Printers and Faxes window.

To manually install a printer, follow these steps:

1. Open the Control Panel.

2. Open the Printers and Faxes icon.

3. Choose File⇨Add Printer.

   This step starts the Add Printer Wizard.

4. Click the Next button.

5. Choose the option labeled Local Printer Attached to This Computer, and don't check the option labeled Automatically Detect and Install My Plug and Play Printer.

   If you truly have a Plug and Play printer, it would have been installed already.

6. Click the Next button.

7. Select the proper printer port.

   LPT1 is selected. This option is standard and probably the best.

8. Click the Next button.

9. Select your printer's manufacturer from the scrolling list on the left, and then select the specific printer from the scrolling list on the right.

   If you cannot find your printer, the best thing to do is to try to locate the manufacturer on the Web. From that Web page, download the proper printer drivers for Windows XP so that you can use the manufacturer's printer.

10. Click the Next button.

11. Optionally, type a new name for the printer.

12. Click the Next button.

13. Click the Next button again; the sharing options aren't impor-tant now.

14. To print a test page, click the Yes option and then the Next button.

15. Click the Finish button.

In a few seconds, you can observe the test page that's printed. If the test page doesn't print, check the connection and ensure that the printer is on-line or selected and ready to print. Try again. Or, click the Troubleshoot button in the dialog box to begin a troubleshooting session.

## Adding a printer elsewhere on the network

Windows XP is very smart about networking and shared printers. If any printers are available for use on the network, they automatically show up in the Printers and Faxes window. Software to control those printers is also automatically installed on your computer.

## Using a second printer

Windows allows you to use any number of printers, printers either directly connected to your computer or to computers on a network. You can easily attach a second printer to your computer by using a second LPT port (LPT2 — if the console has one), or multiple printers by using the USB port and USB expansion hubs.

# The Default Printer

Though you can use multiple printers in Windows, one of the printers must be set up as your main printer. This is what Windows calls the *default printer.*

The default printer is the one that Windows uses to print when you don't select another printer or when printing is automatic and you have no opportunity to select another printer.

The default printer is identified in the Printer and Faxes window with a small black circle and a check mark by its icon.

You can have only one default printer at a time, but you can change the default printer. To set a default printer, click the printer's icon in the Printer and Faxes window and then choose File⇨Set As Default Printer from the menu.

# Envelopes

You can print envelopes just as you print any other piece of paper by using your computer and printer. The trick is to think of the envelope as nothing more than a specially sized sheet of paper. When you get that down, printing on an envelope is easy.

## Configuring your document as an envelope

To set up a document as an envelope, you use the common File⇨Page Setup command, or whichever command the application uses to format a page in a document.

The File⇨Page Setup command summons a Page Setup dialog box. In that or a similar dialog box, choose Envelope #10 as the paper size. Usually, this option is found on a drop-down list. (Note that you can select other special paper sizes as well, and perhaps even enter custom envelope sizes.) Click OK and the document is properly set up to be printed as an envelope.

## Printing on an envelope on the printer

Most printers have a special location to input an envelope. On some printers, it may be a special slot. On other printers, you may simply adjust the paper input guides to a very narrow setting to accommodate the envelope. Regardless, most printers have markings on them to indicate where and how the envelope must be inserted.

Be careful to note the envelope's orientation. Because it's easy to improperly insert an envelope, I recommend doing a test printing first. That way, you can determine whether to insert the envelope face up or face down, and which edge of the envelope goes in first, long or short.

When you have determined which way to insert the envelope, I recommend that you attach a note to the printer or draw on the printer directly with a Sharpie or other pen, to remind you of which way the envelope goes. You can use one of the icons in the following figure as a guide.

Choose one of the icons to represent how your printer accepts envelopes, and then draw something similar in the proper location on your printer (if such a thing doesn't already exist).

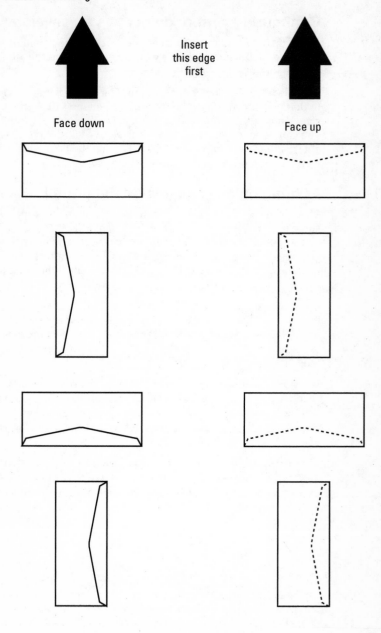

Insert this edge first

Face down

Face up

# Ink and Toner

Two consumable items required by your computer's printer are ink and paper. Ink is necessary to throw the image down on the paper. A pencil without lead is a stick. A printer without ink is an expensive door stop.

✔ Inkjet printers need ink cartridges.

✔ Laser printers need toner cartridges.

✔ Older-style printers required printer ribbons.

You have to refer to your printer's manual for specifics on removing and adding ink or toner. Note that sometimes the instructions are easily found right under the printer's lid.

## Ink cartridges

Inkjet printers use from one to six ink cartridges, depending on the type of printer. Ink cartridges come in these types:

✔ Black ink only

✔ Multicolor: yellow, blue, and red ink

✔ Multicolor: two yellow inks, two red inks, and blue or cyan ink

✔ Individual colors

How your inkjet printer uses ink cartridges depends on the printer's price and purpose. For example, professional color-photo printers use six ink colors (including black). Some cheaper ink printers just use three colors and no black ink.

When a color cartridge is empty — even if it's just one color in a multicolor cartridge — the entire thing must be replaced. That's why it's better to get an ink printer that has separate cartridges, one for each color.

Yes, ink cartridges are expensive!

## Toner

Just like copy machines, laser printers use toner cartridges as their inky substance. The toner cartridges aren't cheap! Fortunately, you can get more pages of paper from a single laser printer toner cartridge than an inkjet printer gets from a single thimble of ink.

Color laser printers require up to five toner cartridges, one each for black, magenta, cyan, and yellow, plus an extra black toner cartridge just because.

## Ink and toner tips

- ✔ Remember the cartridge or toner part number for your printer! Not all ink or toner cartridges are alike; they're not interchangeable.

- ✔ I recommend buying the brand-name ink cartridges, despite their extra cost.

- ✔ Keep spare toner or ink cartridges available. Whenever I buy a new cartridge, I buy two. That way, when I run out, I don't need to rush to the store right away.

- ✔ Change the ink or toner when it gets low. Do not delay. Do it at once. Failure to do so can damage your printer.

- ✔ When you first see the toner-low signal from your laser printer, you can squeeze a few more pages from it (an exception to the preceding rule). Remove the toner cartridge from the printer and gently rock it back and forth to redistribute the ink powder. Reinsert the cartridge into the printer. The next time the toner-low signal appears, however, you must replace the toner; this trick works only once.

- ✔ Yes, you can use those toner-recharging places, which is cheaper than buying new toner from the manufacturer. Ditto for ink refilling, but ensure that it's quality stuff you're getting.

- ✔ You don't always have to print in color. You can save ink on an inkjet printer by printing test images in grayscale rather than full color all the time.

# *Paper*

After ink, the second replaceable item you need in order to keep your printer happy is paper. Printers eat paper. You need to be sure that you buy your printer the proper types of paper to keep it happy — and there are several types of paper you can use, and many types to avoid.

## Buying paper

The best kind of paper for your printer is sold with the printer type right on the paper package. For example, inkjet printer paper says "Inkjet printer paper" right on the package. Ditto for laser printer paper, though for a laser printer any photocopier paper does just as well.

Specialty papers abound for computer printers, from high-quality ink paper that really absorbs inkjet printer ink to photo and glossy photo paper to transparencies and even iron-on transfers. Always ensure that the specialty paper works with your printer.

## Adding paper to the printer

Computer printers accept paper in one of two ways: The paper is either stacked up inside a tray, similar to a copy machine, or set in a feeding bin.

When the printer runs out of paper, it lets you know, either via a message on the computer screen or some message on the printer's control panel.

Yes, there's a face-up and face-down way of inserting paper into a printer. This distinction is important only when the paper manufacturer recommends that you print on one side of the paper first, or when you're printing on both sides of a sheet of paper. Directions on the printer should tell you which side of the paper is printed first. If not, feel free to borrow the icons in the following figure.

## Paper tips

✔ Keep your printer supplies, including the paper, near your printer for easy access.

✔ Buy plenty of paper for your printer! Stock up! Paper is cheaper by the box. Try to find a discount, bulk-paper dealer near you.

✔ Be careful to note which side of the paper needs to be printed on first — if that's the case.

✔ Not all inkjet printer paper works in laser printers. For example, if the photo paper says that it's for a color laser printer, it probably works just fine. But, if the paper doesn't say that it's okay for a color laser printer, it doesn't work.

✔ Avoid using powdered or erasable bond paper in your computer printer. The powder gums up the works.

✔ Paper stock that's too thick may not be able to wend its way through your printer's internals. I generally stick with 25-pound stock as the thickest paper to use in a computer printer.

✔ For the best printing on a laser printer, I recommend getting laser paper.

✔ That continuous fanfold paper you may have seen in old movies or photos is for older impact (dot-matrix) printers that you will probably never use.

✔ Some printers are capable of handling larger-size paper, such as legal or tabloid. If yours can use these sizes, make sure that you load the paper properly and tell Windows or your software application that you're using a different size of paper.

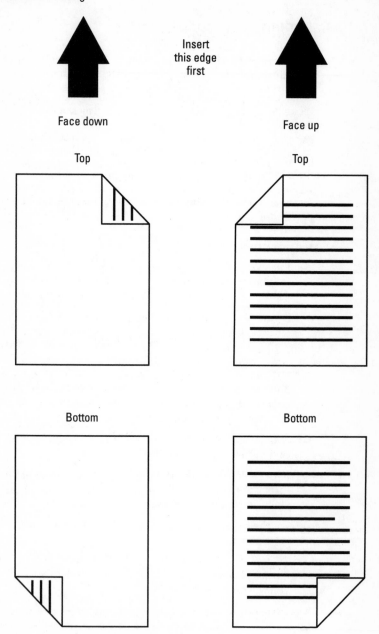

Insert this edge first

# The Printer's Control Panel

The printer is really a computer all its own. Some printers have full-on microprocessors and their own memory. Other printers — cheap ones — use the computer for most of the computing horse-power, but printers still remain complex and interesting gizmos. As such, each printer has a control panel.

On some printers, the control panel is a small LCD screen with buttons to scroll through various menus and select options. Other printers may have just one or two buttons that control everything — beyond the basic power button.

Here are a few key things to locate on the printer's control panel:

✓ **Power button and light.**

✓ **Paper-out light.** This may also appear as a warning on the printer's LCD screen.

✓ **Ink/toner out/low light.** This message may also appear on the LCD screen. There may be different lights for the different ink cartridges.

✓ **The on-line or select button.** Some printers require that an on-line or select button be pressed before the printer communi-cates with the computer. This button isn't used to turn the printer off and on, but rather open or close communications with the printer. For example, you deselect or take the printer off-line to change ink cartridges or eject a page or fix a misfeed.

✓ **Stop or Cancel.** This button is used to immediately halt print-ing. Consider yourself fortunate if your printer sports one of these babies.

✓ **The form-feed button.** This button ejects a sheet of paper from the printer.

# Printing

In the computer world, printed material is called *hard copy*, and it's often the last step in creating something with the computer. The hard copy is pass-around proof of your efforts, the paper you turn in, a list to take shopping, sheet music for others to play, pictures to look at — you name it. Getting it on paper is what the printer is all about.

## The Print command

Printing is the same in nearly every Windows application. Here are the steps I recommend that you take to print your creation:

*1.* Save your stuff!

Always save before you print. It's a good habit.

*2.* Turn on the printer (if necessary).

Or, take whatever steps to ensure that the printer is on-line and ready to print.

*3.* Choose File⇨Print.

The keyboard shortcut is Ctrl+P.

*4.* Make any necessary adjustments in the Print dialog box.

The majority of these adjustments are covered in the remainder of this section.

*5.* Click the Print button to print the document.

*6.* Remove the document from the printer.

 You can also print by clicking a Print toolbar button. Note that the button often just prints the document immediately without first displaying a Print dialog box.

## Choosing a printer

When your computer is connected to multiple printers, such as printers on a network, you select a printer inside the Print dialog box. There, you see either a list of icons or a drop-down list of printer descriptions.

When you don't choose a printer, such as when you click the Print toolbar button, Windows uses the *default printer.*

## Selecting paper size

Paper size is sometimes chosen in the Print dialog box, but most often a File⇨Page Setup command is used to set the paper size instead. The paper size is set by either selecting from a list of preset sizes or manually entering a new size — depending on the program being used.

Choosing new paper in the program also requires that you feed the proper paper size into your printer. Some printers have a wide slot available to accommodate just about any size of paper. Otherwise, the paper must fit into a special tray, such as with a laser printer.

Remember to load the printer with the proper size of paper before you print!

## Printing in color or grayscale

One way to save on color ink is to print test documents using *grayscale,* or shades of gray (black ink), rather than color. This setting is made in different places, depending on the printer.

Depending on your printer setup or the application you're using, you may have to summon the Print dialog box and click an Advanced, Effects, or Properties button. Then, you must hunt through the various dialog boxes for a Grayscale command or option that sets the output to use black ink only.

For example, you may have to click the Properties button in the Print dialog box to display the Printer's Properties dialog box. Then, click a Color tab. Then, put a check mark by the Use Grayscale option. Click OK to set up the printer, and then click the Print button to print.

The grayscale setting typically works only once; you have to make that setting or change it again to print the next document in grayscale as well.

## Printing one page from many

Some Print dialog boxes allow you to specify which pages of a document to print. There may be buttons to select all odd pages, all even pages, or the entire document. Or, there may be a text box where you can enter individual pages or a range of pages.

To print an individual page, simply specify that page in the text box:

5

To print a range of pages, use the hyphen to separate the first and last pages in the range:

2-10

To print a smattering of pages, separate them with commas:

5, 13-15, 19, 23-30

## Printing sideways

The official lingo involved with printing sideways is *landscape mode.* Normally, printing is done in *portrait mode,* where the paper is short on top and long on the sides. Landscape mode is where the printing goes longways on a page.

The option to set Portrait or Landscape is usually found in the Page Setup dialog box, not in the Print dialog box. To make that setting, choose File⇨Page Setup. Sometimes, the command is in the main part of the dialog box, or you may have to click a Layout or Paper tab.

 It's best to choose Landscape mode before you start creating your document because other commands — margins, graphics size, and position — are affected by this change.

Note that printing sideways is done by the printer's software. You don't need to load the paper sideways for it to work.

## Print Preview

To help save paper, and to give you a good idea of what the printed document will look like, most applications come with a Print Preview command. This command simply shows you onscreen exactly what the printed document looks like, all the way up to the edge of the paper.

 The Print Preview command is commonly found on the File menu. A Print Preview toolbar button can also be used.

Most applications don't let you edit text or modify your document in Print Preview mode. You must first close the Print Preview window or somehow return to editing mode to continue working on the document.

# Printing the Screen

It's possible to get a printed copy of what you see on the screen, or of a single window. This trick is complicated, but it can be done. Pay close attention:

*1.* Arrange the screen so that it looks the way you want to see it printed, or ensure that the single window you want to capture is "on top of" all other windows.

*2.* Press the Print Screen key to capture the entire screen, or press Alt+Print Screen to capture just a window.

The image is now copied into the Windows Clipboard. From there, you can paste it into any program that accepts graphics.

*3.* From the Start button's menu, choose All Programs⇨ Accessories⇨Paint to start the Windows Paint program.

4. Choose Edit⇨Paste.

   The screen image is now pasted into the Paint program, from which you can print.

   You can optionally save the image at this point, if necessary.

5. Choose File⇨Print.

   Make necessary adjustments in the Print dialog box, and ensure that the printer is ready to print.

6. Click the Print button to print the screen.

7. Quit Paint when you're done.

## Printing a Test Page

One way to ensure that the printer is working and on speaking terms with the computer is to print a test page. This is done initially when you set up any printer for the first time, but Windows lets you print a test page again, just to ensure that everything is working:

1. Open the Printers and Faxes window.

   This window can be found by opening the Printers and Faxes icon in the Control Panel.

2. Right-click the printer's icon.

3. Choose Properties from the pop-up menu.

4. Click the button labeled Print Test Page.

## Stopping the Printer

In those moments when your patience flits away, or when something trots off to the printer before its time, you need to stop printing, by canceling the printing *jobs* before paper spews all over the place.

The easiest way to stop printing is to locate a Cancel or Stop button on the printer's control panel. That generally stops the printing, by canceling the current page and halting any further information from coming into the printer.

If your printer lacks a Cancel or Stop button, or if you're printing a large document and you want to ensure that it's fully purged from memory, take these steps:

1. Locate the tiny printer icon in the system tray.

   If you can see this guy, great. Otherwise, you have to open the Printers and Faxes window and locate your printer's icon.

2. Open the printer icon.

   The printer's queue dialog box is displayed and lists the document that's currently printing plus any documents waiting to be printed.

3. Choose Printer⇨Cancel All Documents.

   This step stops everything. That's probably what you want. Fix the problem, and then print again.

## Turning the Printer On and Off

Like other computer peripherals, printers have an on–off switch. Unlike the console, it's a *real* on–off switch, not a power button; clicking the off button really does turn the printer off, and right away.

Most modern printers can be left on all the time. The printers have a special sleep, or standby, mode, just like computers do. After a while, printers enter this mode, where they use little or no power and essentially turn themselves off. When the signal comes in to start printing, the printer automatically wakes itself up and prints. Then, it goes back to sleep after a period of inactivity.

You can turn your printer off, if you like. Just flip the switch. But, remember to turn the printer on again before printing.

## Types of Printers

All printers serve the job of giving you a hard copy. Specifically, two popular types of computer printers are available on the market: inkjet printers and laser printers.

You can still find the old dot-matrix, or impact, printers. They're used for high-speed operations, such as printing invoices or filling in forms. Individual computer users don't need them, mostly because they're very slow when printing graphics and everything in Windows is graphics.

### Inkjet printers

The inkjet printer uses literally a jet of ink to create an image on paper. A tiny ink ball is lobbed from the inkjet nozzle directly onto the paper. The ball is small enough that it's nearly instantly absorbed by the paper (though better paper absorbs the ink more efficiently).

Inkjet printers take advantage of several different inks, up to six in a single printer. The more ink, the more realistic the images. For example, special color-photo ink printers use up to six ink colors to create near-photographic-like quality in their output.

The chief advantage of inkjet printers is that they're relatively inexpensive and they generate cheap color output.

The main disadvantage of inkjet printers is that the replacement cost of the ink cartridges is *not* cheap. In fact, it's often said that manufacturers give away the printer and make up the cost by selling you ink.

## Laser printers

The technology behind the laser printer is the same as is found in a photocopier. But, rather than create an image by reflecting light off an original, a laser beam etches the printed image on a magnetic drum, which then sucks up toner dust and literally fuses the toner dust to the paper to create an image.

Laser printers are generally more expensive than inkjet printers, but then again, they're the workhorses of the modern computerized office. They're faster than inkjet printers, and the quality is higher.

Though color laser printers are available, the quality and cost of ink printers make them more attractive for individuals.

# Uninstalling a Printer

Removing a printer from your computer system involves both hardware and software duties.

On the hardware side, simply disconnect the printer from the console; unplug the printer or USB cable.

On the software side, open the Printers and Faxes window. Select your printer's icon, and then choose File⇨Delete from the menu. If you're prompted, I recommend that you leave the printer's software installed on your computer. That way, if you need to use the printer later, you don't have to reinstall the software.

You cannot remove a network printer. For that printer to be removed, it must be uninstalled on the computer to which it's connected, or it must be disconnected from the network.

# Networking

Networking was once a complex and detailed thing, found exclusively in large businesses or universities and under the control of immortal computer experts and other high deities. That same complex and detailed networking is now available for computers in your own home or small office. Nothing much has changed, other than a lack of immediate access to the networking deities. Yep: Networking is possible, and very useful, but taming the network is now a job done by mere mortals. The information in this part should help.

## In this part ...

# About Networking

Networking allows multiple computers to share resources, such as files, printers, and modems. If you have more than one computer, you can network them. That way, you can share information between them, share a single printer, or share a high-speed Internet connection.

Like everything else in a computer, networking is accomplished by a combination of hardware and software.

Networking hardware requires a NIC, or network information card, which is an Ethernet hardware adapter. This item comes either as an expansion card or as part of the motherboard. Most new PCs, and all laptops, come with networking hardware.

Windows provides all the networking software you need. (You may need a specific software driver for the NIC, but beyond that, Windows does just about everything.)

# Accessing Another Computer

Windows XP is good about listing all of a computer's shared resources on the network. You find shared folders in the My Network Places window and shared printers in any Printer dialog box. Yet, if you still want to access another computer on the network directly, or just see a list of all computers in your workgroup, follow these steps:

1. Open the My Network Places icon on the desktop to display the My Network Places window.

2. From the Network Tasks pane (on the left), click the item labeled View Workgroup Computers.

3. Double-click a computer's icon to view any shared resources on that computer.

Not every computer on the network is sharing resources.

Linux and Mac computers on the network must be configured properly before you can access those systems from your PC.

Only computers in your workgroup are shown in the window. To see other workgroups, and view computers belonging to those workgroups, click the Up button or press the Backspace key on your keyboard.

# Accessing a Shared Folder

Shared folders are listed in the My Network Places window. Windows XP automatically searches for any folder on any other Windows computer that is "up for grabs." That folder is then listed in the My Network Places window in the Local Network area.

 To view the My Network Places window, open the My Network Places icon on the desktop. This window's contents can also be accessed from any folder list or Address bar drop-down list.

 There's a shortcut to the My Network Places window in every Save As or Open dialog box. Click the My Network Places button on the left side of the window.

Shared folder icons appear with "plumbing" beneath them. The folder name also tells you on which computer the folder is located.

In this figure, the folder named `prog` is being shared on the networking computer named Test Monster. The computer's network name is Vishnu.

# Adding a Shared Folder to Your Disk System

For convenience, Windows lets you access, or *map*, a shared folder from another computer to a disk drive letter on your own computer system. That makes accessing the folder work just like accessing another disk drive on your computer. Windows even remembers mapped folders and reassigns them when you restart your computer.

## Mapping a folder to a disk drive

To add a shared folder on the network to your PC's disk drive system, follow these steps:

*1.* Open any Windows Explorer window, such as the My Network Places window.

*2.* Choose Tools⇨Map Network Drive.

The Map Network Drive dialog box appears.

3. Choose a drive letter from the Drive drop-down list.

Try to make the letter memorable, such as Drive R for an archive folder, or drive P for shared *p*hotos.

4. Click the Browse button to locate a shared folder on the network.

The folders appear on the scrolling list, near the bottom. You can choose those folders specifically or choose any subfolder inside a shared folder.

5. Select a folder and click the OK button.

The folder's officially cryptic network name appears in the Folder box.

6. Click to put a check mark by the box labeled Reconnect at Logon.

7. Click the Finish button to add the folder as a mapped disk drive.

The shared folder or disk drive window then appears. (You can close it.)

The mapped drive also appears in the My Computer window.

Some firewalls disable access to folders shared on the local network. If you're using a firewall, be sure to allow access through the firewall (both in and out) from computers on your network.

## Unmapping a folder

When you tire of having the convenience of a network drive, you can unmap it. It's cinchy:

1. Open the Windows Explorer window or any folder window.

2. Choose Tools⇨Disconnect Network Drive.

3. Select the icon of the mapped drive you want to disconnect.

4. Click OK.

You may be warned if the connection is still active. If so, stop using the mapped drive, and then try again.

# *Checking the Network Connection*

There are several ways you can confirm that your PC is actively connected to the network and things are set up properly.

## Checking the My Network Places window

Opening the My Network Places icon displays a list of shared resources that are accessible over the network. If you open that icon and the window is empty, it means either that networking isn't working or that there just aren't any resources to be shared.

## Checking the Network Connections window

The Network Connections window displays a list of networking hardware available to your computer. See also "The Network Connections Window."

In the Network Connections window, locate the icon representing the local-area connection. Open that icon to display a dialog box listing the status of the connection. The Status should read "Connected," and the Activity area of the dialog box should list a goodly amount of bytes both sent and received.

You can also click the Support tab to ensure that a valid IP address has been issued. (A *valid* IP address consists of some numbers other than all zeroes.) Note that a Repair button is located on the Support tab, to help troubleshoot the network connection.

## Using the little networking guys

When your PC is actively connected to a network, the little networking-guys icon appears in the system tray, to tell you that the networking is happening.

Double-clicking the networking guys displays the network status dialog box, which can also be displayed from the Network Connections window, as covered in the preceding subsection.

## Displaying the little networking guys

To ensure that the little networking guys appear in the system tray, follow these steps:

*1.* Click to select the Local Area Connection icon in the Network Connections window.

See also "The Network Connections Window."

*2.* Choose File⇨Properties to display the connection's Properties dialog box.

*3.* Click to put a check mark by the item labeled Show Icon in Notification Area When Connected.

*4.* Click OK.

# Connecting to the Network

The only good news about connecting to a computer network is that after you get it right, you never really have to do it again. It's getting to that point that causes the most frustration among PC users.

## The NIC

On the hardware side of connecting the network, your PC needs a NIC, or network interface card. This item is an adapter that plugs into one of the expansion slots on your PC, or the hardware can be included on the motherboard. Either way, the result is an RJ-45 jack, or network hole, on the console's rump.

You may also need to install software for your NIC. This isn't networking software, but rather a software *driver* that controls the NIC and interfaces it with the rest of your PC's hardware.

## The network cable

Physically connecting the network is networking cable, also known as *Cat-5 cable*. This cable connects each computer on the network to a central router, switch, or networking hub.

The ends of the cable are RJ-45 jacks, one of which plugs into the NIC on your PC and the other of which plugs into the router, switch, or hub.

You can also network two PCs directly, by connecting a network cable between each computer's NIC.

## Configuring the network

After making the hardware connection, your next step is to properly configure Windows to understand and obey the network. This is best done by running the Network Setup Wizard:

1. Open the My Network Places icon on the desktop to display the My Network Places window.

2. From the left side of the window, choose the task labeled Set Up a Home or Small Office Network.

3. Answer the questions given by the Network Setup Wizard, and click the Next button after each choice.

4. Click the Finish button when the wizard is done.

## Connecting to a Wireless Network

Wireless networking is all the rage. As long as your PC is equipped with a wireless networking adapter and a broadcast networking signal is available, you too can do the networking thing without wires.

The best way to connect to a wireless network is to have your networking manager set things up for you. This strategy is ideal for situations in which your computer is permanently located. For cybercafés or airports or other locations you may visit, use the instructions in this part of the book.

The networks are out there! To find them, do this:

1. Open the Network Connections icon in the Control Panel to display the Network Connections window.

2. Right-click the Wireless Network Connection icon.

3. Choose View Available Wireless Networks.

4. Click to select a name, or SSID, from the list of available wireless networks.

5. Enter the WEP, or wireless network's password, in the Network Key box.

   The password must be typed *exactly!* Upper- and lowercase are different! Note that some passwords can be quite long.

6. Retype the same password into the Confirm Network Key box.

7. Click the Connect button.

If the connection is made, a pop-up bubble appears and informs you of the wireless networking status, speed, and other stuff.

Not every network has a password, but I highly recommend using only those networks that are password protected. When you use a non-password-protected network, Windows complains often and occasionally disconnects you from the network, just to spite you.

## Getting Your PC's IP Address

Every computer on the network has its own, unique network ID number, known as an *IP address*. IP stands for Internet Protocol, the same rules and directions for connecting computers on the Internet. It's pronounced "I pee" as in "I am urinating."

You may be asked to report your PC's IP address for troubleshooting purposes or to tech support. When asked, here's how you can report that information:

*1.* Display the networking status dialog box by double-clicking the networking guys in the system tray or by opening the connection's icon in the Network Connections window.

*2.* Click the Support tab in the dialog box.

The IP address is listed, along with the cryptic values of the subnet mask and default gateway — which should be more than enough for tech support to chew on.

*3.* More detailed (and scary) information can be obtained by clicking the Details button.

Most networks assign IP addresses to all the computers on the network. This is done by using a networking program named DHCP. If your network uses a router or one computer is using Internet Connection Sharing, it provides the IP addresses to all other computers on the network by using DHCP. If not, IP addresses must be manually assigned.

DHCP stands for Dynamic Host Configuration Protocol, if that makes you feel any better.

Most IP addresses for the local network start with either 10.0.*x.x* or 192.168.*x.x*.

## Getting Your PC's MAC Address

The MAC address is a unique number given to your PC's Ethernet hardware. It's different from the IP address in that the MAC address is encoded in hardware and cannot be changed. Many wireless networks use the MAC address as a form of security; no two MAC addresses are identical and it's difficult to fake a MAC address.

To discover your PC's MAC address, follow the steps in the preceding section and click the Details button in Step 3. The MAC address appears as the first item on the list, labeled Physical Address.

If your PC has more than one NIC, each one has its own, distinct MAC address.

MAC stands for Medial Access Control. Say "mack," not the letters.

# The My Network Places Window

 My Network Places is the name of an icon and a window in Windows where shared resources on the network are all listed. To open the window, double-click the My Network Places icon on the desktop. You may also find a link to this folder on the Start button's menu.

 Any folder available for sharing elsewhere on the network appears in the My Network Places window.

The task pane (on the left) of the My Network Places window lists common networking tasks as well as links to other networking locations on your computer.

In previous versions of Windows, My Network Places was named Network Neighborhood.

# The Network Connections Window

Windows keeps your networking hardware, as well as various network connections that are made, in one location, known as the Network Connections window.

 This window can be handy to get to if a link to it appears on the Start button's menu. Otherwise, you get there from the Control Panel's Network Connections icon.

The Network Connections window lists the available networking hardware as well as other connections, split up into different areas, similar to how the My Computer window lists storage devices in categories. The task pane on the left side of the window also contains handy links for adding new network hardware, software, and other networking options.

# The PC's Network Name

All PCs connected to the network make themselves known in various ways:

✔ The computer's IP address

✔ The networking hardware's MAC address

✔ The computer's networking name

✔ The computer's description

✔ Any shared resources on the computer

The computer's networking name is used by Windows to name the computer system as well. So, if Windows knows your computer as Daisy, it also appears on the network as Daisy. This nonsense, along with the computer's description, is changed in the System Properties dialog box:

1. Open the System icon in the Control Panel.

2. Click the Computer Name tab.

3. The text description of your computer is entered in the box labeled Computer Description.

   This text is optional, but the description appears in the My Network Places window.

4. To change the computer's name, click the Change button.

5. Type the name in the Computer Name text box.

   Try to keep the name to fewer than 15 characters, with no spaces. No two computers on the network can share the same name.

6. Click OK to set the new computer name.

   The name appears in the My Network Places window by any shared folders. It also becomes the root name of the computer in a network pathname.

7. Click OK to close the System Properties dialog box and accept your changes.

   Restart Windows if you're prompted to do so.

The My Network Places window lists shared resources on other computers by using this format:

*shared resource name on Computer description (Computer name)*

You also see network paths beginning with two backslashes, followed by the computer name and then the path of the shared resource.

## Sharing a Folder

To make a folder on your computer available to other computers on the network, heed these steps:

1. Click to select the folder.

   That folder and its contents — including any and all subfolders and their contents — are shared on the network.

2. Choose File⇨Sharing and Security.

3. In the folder's Properties dialog box, click to put a check mark by the option labeled Share This Folder on the Network.

   You cannot select this item if the folder is private or one of its parent folders is private.

4. Optionally, enter a Share name.

   This is the folder's name as it appears to others on the network. By specifying a share name, you can apply a more descriptive name to the folder and its contents than the name given the folder on your PC.

5. Optionally, click to put a check mark by the item labeled Allow Network Users to Change My Files.

   If you check this item, others on the network can delete, modify, or add to any files inside the shared folder or any of its subfolders.

6. Click the OK button to share the folder.

I don't recommend that you share the root folder of any hard drive; likewise, don't share any of Windows own folders or folders containing programs you have installed on your computer. Such a thing proves to be a major security risk. (Windows warns you when you try.)

 Shared folders appear with the "serving hand" icon beneath them.

No, you cannot share individual files, only the folders that contain the files. Likewise, compressed folders — which are really only files — cannot be shared individually.

## Sharing an Internet Connection

There's no reason that only one computer in your house should have the high-speed Internet connection. That's just rude! Instead, that single computer can use Windows to share the Internet connection with other computers on the network.

Ideally, what you want is to have the high-speed modem connect to a router, which then connects the rest of the computers on your network. This situation is the best and avoids having to deal with sharing an Internet connection. But, if you're stubborn, you can do this instead:

1. Open the Network Connections icon in the Control Panel to display the Network Connections window.

  2. Click to select the high-speed Internet connection.

     Or, you can select a modem or an ISP's icon from the list.

  3. Choose File➪Properties.

  4. Click the Advanced tab in the connection's Properties dialog box.

  5. Click to put a check mark by the item labeled Allow Other Network Users to Connect Through This Computer's Internet Connection.

  6. Click OK.

Other computers can now find the Internet connection available in their Network Connections window.

To unshare the connection, repeat these steps, but remove the check mark in Step 5.

# Sharing a Printer

To make your printer available for use by others on the network, follow these steps:

  1. Open the Printers and Faxes icon in the Control Panel.

  2. Click to select the printer attached to your computer that you want to share.

  3. Choose File➪Sharing.

  4. In the printer's Properties dialog box, click to select the option labeled Share This Printer.

  5. Optionally, give the printer a name.

     I recommend naming the printer after the type of printer or its location, such as Color Laser in the Den or Photo Printer in Production.

  6. Click OK.

Printers you're sharing appear with the serving-hand icon beneath their icon, just like shared folders on your computer.

# Unsharing a Folder

Folders remain up for grabs as long as you want, or until you elect to unshare them. This is cinchy:

  1. Click to select the shared folder.

2. Choose File⇨Sharing and Security.

3. In the folder's Properties dialog box, click to remove the check mark by the option labeled Share This Folder on the Network.

4. Click OK.

If someone else on the network is using the folder, you're warned about breaking the connection.

## Unsharing a Printer

To keep that printer all for yourself — indeed, to hide its usefulness from the rest of the dweebs on the network — do this:

1. Open the Printers and Faxes icon in the Control Panel to display the Printers and Faxes window.

2. Click to select the shared printer.

3. Choose File⇨Sharing.

4. Click to select the option labeled Do Not Share This Printer.

5. Click OK.

## Using a Network Printer

See Part VIII for more information about printing over the network.

## Workgroups

The simplest type of network is the *peer-to-peer* network. In this setup, the network lacks a central powerful computer, such as a file server. Instead, each computer can access any other computer on the network directly. To help keep the network organized, it can further be broken up into smaller units, called workgroups.

A *workgroup* is nothing more than a collection of computers on the network. By isolating larger networks into workgroups, it makes accessing other computers with similar needs and resources easier. But, on a small office or home office system, workgroups are still necessary, even though the system doesn't have that many computers.

Your computer must belong to a workgroup so that you can easily access other computers in the workgroup. For a small office or home office, I recommend that all computers belong to the same workgroup.

Only resources from the workgroup appear in the My Network Places window.

## Creating and joining a workgroup

To join a workgroup, you simply specify its name:

1. Open the System icon in the Control Panel.

2. Click the Computer Name tab in the System dialog box.

3. Click the Change button to display the Computer Name Changes dialog box.

4. In the Member Of area, choose the option labeled Workgroup.

5. Type the name of the workgroup.

   Either enter the name of an existing workgroup or create a new name for your workgroup here. For example, my computers are on a workgroup named CAT. All the computers specify CAT as the workgroup name; therefore, they all belong to that workgroup.

   The workgroup name should be short, with no spaces.

6. Click OK to close the Computer Name Changes dialog box.

7. Click OK to dismiss the System Properties dialog box.

   Restart Windows if you're prompted to do so.

## Viewing the workgroup computers

To view all computers belonging to the workgroup, open the My Network Places window. Then, choose the task (on the left side of the window) labeled View Workgroup Computers.

When a computer is turned off, disconnected from the network, or not a member of the workgroup, it doesn't show up in the window.

When the workgroup window is empty, it means that your computer is the only member of its workgroup. Otherwise, you have misspelled the workgroup name or have some other network problem.

If you click the Up arrow when you're viewing the workgroup, you display another window, which lists all workgroups on the network. Click the Up arrow again, and you see any networks available to your computer displayed in the window.

# Creating Your Own CDs

It has been a tradition that folks want to both read from and write to their removable computer media. Blame it on the floppy disk. So, when CDs first started holding computer data, folks wondered why they couldn't write data to the disk. Alas, it was a CD-ROM, where the RO means Read-Only. Writing to a CD just wasn't happening. That was more than ten years ago.

Many PCs are now blessed with a CD drive that both reads from and writes to CDs. By using such a drive, you can create your own data or music CD. Windows comes with all the software you need. You just buy the right kind of discs, and soon you'll be a CD-burning fool.

(Many PCs also come with DVD drives that can read and write information to DVD discs. This book doesn't cover that topic because the software required in order to record on a DVD is unique to the drive. When Windows itself has the ability to write to a DVD disc, this book will be updated to cover writing to DVD discs as well as to CDs.)

## In this part . . .

# CD Types

There are two types of CDs on which you can record information:

✔ CD-R, or CD recordable

✔ CD-RW, or CD rewriteable

Be careful to note that some CD drives record only CD-Rs. Even so, most modern PCs have CD-R drives that can record on both types of discs, CD-R and CD-RW.

Like a CD, both disc formats can store from 640MB to 720MB of information, depending on the disc.

## The CD-R

You can write information only once to a CD-R disc. After the disc is full, it cannot be written to again, although it can be read from. Nearly all computers recognize the CD-R format and can read from that type of disc, even if the drive is a standard (not recording) CD.

Data is *burned* to the CD-R before the disc is ejected. But, in Windows, that doesn't mean that you're done with the disc. You can reinsert the disc and continue to add information until it's full.

Information can be written to the CD-R in short spurts or in one long burst.

There are specialized CD-R discs for data and for music. Be sure that you buy the proper type! Buying the discs in bulk (on a spool) is the least expensive way to go.

## The CD-RW

CD-RW discs work exactly like CD-R discs. The main difference is that you can completely erase the disc and use it all over again, as though it were new or empty.

Note that CD-RW discs don't allow you to delete information from the disc in small chunks or individually. Instead, the whole disc must be erased at one time. Aside from that, the CD-RW works exactly like a CD-R disc.

CD-RW discs aren't well-suited for recording music. Not all audio CD players are compatible with the CD-RW format.

Finally, CD-RW discs are more expensive than CD-Rs, which makes their usefulness questionable. After all, it's cheaper to buy a few CD-Rs and use them than to keep reusing a CD-RW.

# Checking to See Whether You Have a CD-R/RW Drive

Examining your PC's CD drive solves the mystery of whether you can create your own CDs. The drive itself says "Recordable," plus maybe "Rewriteable," right on the front.

Some customized computers may not have CD drives with text on them. In that case, you can check the My Computer window to see whether the drive is listed as a CD-R or CD-RW.

Finally, you can check the CD drive's Properties dialog box for a Recording tab. See also "Enabling a CD-R/RW Drive."

# Creating a Musical CD

You can use the Windows Media Player program to create musical CDs. The music can come from the Internet or from other CDs you own. The Media Player program lets you build collections of music in *playlists*. You can then burn the playlists to CDs for playback in any CD player.

Other programs exist that let you burn music CDs, but the Windows Media Player comes standard with Windows. The following sections are specific to Windows Media Player; other programs use similar steps, so you can follow along here if you're using one of the many CD-music-creation programs.

## Building a playlist

The first step to create a musical CD is to build a *playlist,* or a collection of songs grouped together so that they can all be written to a single CD. These steps are for the Windows Media Player; the steps in other media programs should be similar:

1. Press Ctrl+N to create a new playlist.

2. Type a name for the new playlist.

3. Click OK.

4. Select your playlist beneath the My Playlists heading, on the left side of the Media Player window.

   You may need to click the + (plus sign) by the My Playlists heading to display all your playlists.

5. Choose All Music from the left side of the Media Player window.

6. Drag songs from the right side of the window to your playlist on the left side.

Repeat Step 6 as you build the playlist.

Remember that there's a size limit on how much music fits on a CD. Depending on the CD, it can be 70 minutes or more. Every so often, select all the songs in your playlist and look at the Total Time value, near the bottom of the window.

### Burning a playlist

The Windows Media Player creates music CDs by burning a playlist to the CD. You must first create a playlist, or a collection of music, and then insert a blank CD-R — preferably one specially created for holding music, into the CD drive. Then, follow these steps in Media Player after inserting the disc:

1. Click the button on the left labeled Copy to CD or Device.

2. Choose your playlist from the drop-down menu atop the left side of the window.

   The playlist menu button is located beneath the text Items to Copy.

3. Click the Copy button in the upper-right part of the window.

   The songs are converted in the proper format for a music CD and then burned to the CD-R. The time taken depends on the speed of the CD-R drive.

After the last song is written, Windows closes the disc, which means that no more files or music can be written to it. The disc, however, can be played in any CD player or computer CD drive.

## Destroying a CD

CD-Rs can be thrown away, but that means not only that anyone can still read the data, but that there may also be rules in your community about disposing of CDs.

CDs can be considered as hazardous waste because when they burn, they emit noxious fumes. Don't burn your CDs to destroy them!

If you really want to properly dispose of a CD or CD-R disc, obtain a CD shredder. It works like a paper shredder — and may indeed double as a paper shredder — effectively rendering CDs into small enough bits that only the most diehard spy would be willing to reassemble the thing.

# *Enabling a CD-R/RW Drive*

You need to tell Windows that the CD-R drive is available and ready for recording CDs. This is done in the drive's Properties dialog box:

1. Open the My Computer icon on the desktop, to display the My Computer window.

2. Select your PC's CD-R drive.

   CD-R drives sport no special icon and look just like regular CD drives in the My Computer window.

3. Choose File⇨Properties from the menu.

4. In the drive's Properties dialog box, click the Recording tab.

   Having no Recording tab means that your PC doesn't have a CD-R drive. Or, your drive manufacturer may have its own tab specific to recording on that one drive.

5. Click to put a check mark by the option labeled Enable CD Recording on This Drive.

6. Click OK.

   Optionally, close the My Computer window as well.

# *Erasing a CD-RW*

The only advantage of a CD-RW over a CD-R is that you have the option of completely erasing the disc and starting over. Yes, erasing the disc utterly deletes any files, folders, programs, and whatnot on that disc. But you get to start over again, with a fresh, blank CD-RW, which is the selling point.

To utterly zap a CD-RW, open the disc's window; use the My Computer window to locate the CD drive icon, and open that icon to display the window.

To erase the disc, choose File⇨Erase This CD-RW. This action runs a wizard; click the Next button. That's it.

Windows keeps the disc in the drive, and presents the disc's folder window again, ready for new files to be added.

# *Importing Music*

In Windows, the Media Player program can be used to read a musical CD. The music can be played, but it can also be *imported* into the computer, for storage or for later burning to create a custom CD. (Other programs can be used as well, but Media Player is included with Windows.)

The easiest way to import music is to simply stick a musical CD into the computer's CD drive. If the Autoplay window appears, choose the option that reads Copy Music from CD. That automatically imports all the songs from all the tracks on the CD into Windows Media Player.

When the Autoplay option isn't working, you can do this:

1. Insert the music CD into the computer's CD drive.

   It can be a CD or CD-R drive or even a DVD drive.

2. Start the Windows Media Player program.

   Its icon dwells on the desktop, Quick Launch bar, or Start menu, or it can be found by choosing All Programs➪ Accessories➪Entertainment➪Windows Media Player.

3. Click the item labeled Copy from CD.

   It's on the left side of the Media Player window. Or, if you can see the menu, choose File➪Copy➪Copy from Audio CD and then choose the name of the CD from the submenu.

4. Click the Copy Music button, located at the top of the Media Player window.

   The music is copied one track at a time, and the speed depends on the speed of the CD drive.

The songs that are copied are stored in the Media Player Media Library. Click the Media Library link or choose View➪Go To➪Media Library from the menu to see the imported songs as well as all other media stored and managed by Windows Media Player.

# *Using a CD-R/RW in Windows*

Windows is keenly aware of and understands CD-R and CD-RW discs. If you have the right hardware, Windows lets you add files to those discs in a simple, straightforward manner. Generally, the steps go like this:

✔ Insert the CD-R or CD-RW into the drive.

✔ Direct Windows to open the CD as a writeable folder.

✔ Copy files to the writeable folder.

✔ Burn and eject the CD-R or CD-RW.

Windows uses a special writeable folder to which you can copy — and delete — files. The files sit there until they're written to the CD-R in one blast. That saves on CD disc space.

## Mounting a CD-R or CD-RW

To begin using the CD-R/RW, stick the disc into the drive. Windows recognizes it and asks what to do. Choose the option labeled Open Writeable CD Folder Using Windows Explorer, and click OK. A window for the CD-R/RW disc's drive appears on the screen. The drive is ready for writing.

If Windows doesn't recognize the disc or an error occurs, toss the CD-R/RW out. Bum discs happen. There's nothing you can do, other than throw the turkey away.

## Using a writeable folder

Files aren't written directly to the CD-R/RW. Instead, Windows uses a preparatory window where files sit and wait. That window appears just after you *mount* the CD-R/RW disc. It also shows up when you open the CD's icon in the My Computer window.

To copy a file to the CD-R, it must first be copied to the writeable folder. Do this as you would copy any file from another drive: Choose Edit⇨Copy, Edit⇨Copy to Folder, drag and drop, or any of the file actions covered in Part VI of this book.

There's also a link labeled Copy to CD, which can be found in the task pane of any folder window. You can use that link to copy any selected files to the CD's writeable folder.

Put only copies on the CD-R/RW! Don't use the Save As command to save original work there. Use the CD-R/RW disc for archiving or keeping only copies. You want to use the hard drive for your originals; that's what it's there for.

Files sitting in the writeable folder haven't yet been written to the CD-R/RW. To show that they're waiting, those files appear with a tiny download arrow on their ghosty icon.

If the icon doesn't have the download arrow, the file already has been written to the CD.

## Burning a CD-R/RW

To burn files to the CD, open the CD's writeable folder and choose File⇨Write These Files to CD. This action displays the CD Writing Wizard:

1. Type a name for the CD.

2. Click the Next button.

   Watch as the progress meter keeps you from being bored out of your skull.

The disc is automatically ejected when the writing is complete. It can now be read by any computer with a CD drive.

If there's an error, eject the disc, toss it out, and try with another disc per the directions on the screen.

# Writing to a CD-R/RW a Second (Or Third) Time

You can continue to write to a CD-R or CD-RW until the disc is full. When Windows ejects the disc, it's readable by other computers, although the disc itself has not been "closed" and isn't protected from being written to again. (This may not hold true for other, third-party CD-writing programs.)

To continue writing to a partially written CD-R disc, just stick that disc back into your CD-R drive. Open the drive's window and you see any files already burned to the disc. To add new files, copy them on over.

New files added to the disc appear with the download graphic on their icon. They're sitting in the writeable folder and awaiting burning to the CD. See also "Using a writeable folder."

You can continue to write files to a CD-R or CD-RW until the disc is full.

To get the most from your CD-R, try to write to it all at once. Writing to the disc in small spurts wastes disc space.

# The Keyboard

Hey, that's key-board, not key-bored! How can a computer keyboard be anything but boring, especially with all those buttons? Your PC uses a keyboard as its primary input device. In a way, the keyboard is like the computer's ears. So, forget shouting at your computer — use the keyboard instead!

## In this part . . .

# Accessing Menus with the Keyboard

You can do many things with the keyboard that you can also do with the mouse. Specifically, some folks are keyboard nuts when it comes to accessing menu commands. Although the mouse may seem obvious, those folks argue that the keyboard method is much faster.

To use the keyboard to access menus in Windows, you start by pressing the Alt key. This key displays underlines in the menu names (if they aren't there already). The underlines indicate which keys on the keyboard activate those menu items. From that point onward, it's a matter of pressing the proper keys to match the menu commands.

For example, to access the File⇨Page Setup command in Microsoft Word, you press Alt, F, U. That's Alt to activate the underlines, F for File, and U for Page Setup.

Some manuals and documentation even underline the commands for you to help identify the keys: File⇨Page Setup.

The first step can also be combined: Alt+F, U. In this case, Alt+F immediately accesses the File menu.

Press the Esc key to cancel and back out of the menus.

# The Any Key

The Any key is more of a relic from the computer's text-based past. Oftentimes, a program would prompt you (in what the programmer believed to be a friendly manner) to "Press any key to continue." The idea was to give you a choice: Press any old key on the keyboard, just like a rap on the door to know that things are okay.

Sadly, many beginners would scour the keyboard in futile frustration for a single key labeled Any. There is no such key.

Today, such a message is often more precise: "Press the Enter key to continue." The Enter key *is* the Any key. (Well, and so is the spacebar.)

# Controlling a Window with the Keyboard

The keyboard can be used to manipulate windows on the desktop, though, unlike accessing menus (see the preceding section), this shortcut isn't really faster than using the mouse.

The key to using the keyboard to manipulate a window is understanding the Control menu. All windows have a Control menu, flagged by a tiny icon in the window's upper-left corner. Clicking that icon with the mouse, or pressing Alt+spacebar, displays the Control menu.

Not all Control menus are the same. Some programs have special items, but a few common items are on the Control menu. Some items let you manipulate the window by using the keyboard:

**Restore:** The window is restored to its previous size and location after being maximized.

**Move:** The window can be moved by using the four arrow keys on the keyboard. Simply press an arrow key to move the window in that direction. Press Enter or Esc when you're done moving the window.

**Size:** The window's size can be changed. First, press an arrow key to indicate which side of the window you want to move: right, left, top, or bottom. Then press the corresponding arrow keys to move that side of the window in or out. Press Enter or Esc when you're done.

**Minimize:** The window is minimized and becomes a button on the taskbar.

**Maximize:** The window is maximized to fill the entire screen.

**Close:** The window is closed. If the window is a program, the program quits. The keyboard shortcut to directly access this command is Alt+F4.

# Dead Keys

Certain legacy keys are left over on the PC's keyboard from days gone by. Although some programs may use these, most don't. They exist on the PC's keyboard for compatibility with older programs.

**SysRq.** The System Request key was once considered *the* important operating system key. Sadly, that time never came to pass, although the key has remained on the keyboard, albeit tucked under the Print Screen key.

**Pause.** This key was once used to pause the text display, which was necessary when the PC was an all-text computer. Today, the key may still be used to pause the action in some games, but otherwise it has lost its function.

**Break.** This key was used in the old DOS application to cancel a program, often in conjunction with the Ctrl key. Today, it hides below the Pause key, out of sight and out of mind.

# The Help Key

No Help key is on the PC's keyboard. Instead, in Windows the F1 key is used to summon help. Press F1 in most applications or in Windows itself to bring up a Help window, often specific to whatever action you're doing in a program.

(Help keys were once common on computer keyboards. In fact, the Macintosh computer keyboard sports a key labeled Help.)

# Keyboard Basics

Computer keyboards have evolved through the years, from primitive teletypes to terminals to the standard PC keyboard of today. Even then, the current PC keyboard model, the 104-key keyboard, is only a few years old. And, variations on that keyboard exist from manufacturer to manufacturer, especially on laptop PCs.

## Keyboard layout

Keyboards include these four main areas:

- **Function keys:** These keys, on the top row of the keyboard, are labeled F1 through F12.

- **Typewriter keys:** These are the alphabet and number keys, plus a smattering of punctuation and other symbols — the main part of your computer's keyboard.

- **Cursor-control keys:** Just to the right of the typewriter keys, these keys are used to move a cursor or insertion pointer on the screen, as well as for general editing. The keys are duplicated on the numeric keypad. Some manuals refer to these as the *arrow keys*.

- **Numeric keypad:** This area contains duplicates of the number keys, 0 through 9, along with a period and various mathematical symbols. This area is designed for quick number entry. Also, the numeric keypad doubles as a secondary location for the cursor-control keys. The Num Lock key determines which set of keys — numeric or cursor — are in use. When the Num Lock light is on, the numeric keys are used.

Note that the mathematical symbols surrounding the numeric keypad aren't exactly the ones you learned about in grammar school. Here's a quick translation:

✔ + is for addition.

✔ – is for subtraction.

✔ * is for multiplication.

✔ / is for division.

## Shift keys

Unlike a typewriter, the computer keyboard has three sets of Shift keys. These keys are used in combination with other keys to display interesting characters on the screen, control the cursor, or give commands to the computer:

✔ **Alt:** Short for Alternate Shift key, this key is used in combination with other shift keys or with letter keys to carry out commands or functions in Windows.

✔ **Ctrl:** Also called the *Control* key, this key is used in combination with various letter keys to issue command shortcuts, such as Ctrl+P ("Control pee") to print.

✔ **Shift:** This key works just like the Shift key on a typewriter. Shift is used primarily with the letter keys to produce uppercase text. Shift can also be used with other keys and in combination with other shift keys.

When these keys are used in combination with other keys, a plus sign joins them. For example, Shift+S means to press the Shift and S keys, to yield a capital S on the screen. Ctrl+S is the Save command in many programs. And, a command can even use multiple shift keys, such as Ctrl+Alt+Q.

The Win, or Windows, key can also be used as a shift key.

Occasionally some programs may direct you to press the Shift, Ctrl, or Alt key alone. For example, you press the Alt key alone to activate the menu bar.

Yes, there are two sets of Alt, Ctrl, and Shift keys. You can use either one unless an application directs you to use the left or right key specifically.

## Lock keys

Three Lock keys are on the PC's keyboard, which are also associated with three Lock lights, either above the numeric keypad or on the Lock keys themselves:

✔ **Caps Lock:** Used like Shift-Lock on a typewriter. When this key is active, and the Caps Lock light is on, all alphabet keys on the keyboard generate uppercase letters. But, note that unlike a typewriter, Caps Lock doesn't shift the number keys to their symbols.

✔ **Num Lock:** When this key is active, and the Num Lock light is on, the numeric keypad generates numbers. Otherwise, the numeric keypad is used as a cursor keypad.

✔ **Scroll Lock:** This locking key isn't used in Windows. Only a few spreadsheet programs use it. When Scroll Lock is on, and its light is on, using the cursor keys moves the entire worksheet, not just the cell selector.

See also "Special Keys."

# Keyboard Shortcuts

One of the joys of using a PC keyboard is taking advantage of all the various shortcut keys in Windows because your hands are often resting on the keyboard anyway.

## In a dialog box

| Key | Function |
| --- | --- |
| Alt+↓ | Drop down a list. |
| Alt+letter | Switch to gizmo identified by the underlined letter. |
| Ctrl+Tab | Switch to next tab (multitab dialog boxes). |
| ↓ | Adjust value down, or choose next item in a list. |
| Enter | Click the OK button. |
| Esc | Click the Cancel button. |
| F1 | Display dialog box help. |
| F4 | Display list or drop-down list. |
| Shift+Ctrl+Tab | Switch to preceding tab. |
| Shift+Tab | Switch to preceding input field or dialog box gizmo. |
| Space | Switch check mark off or on. |
| Tab | Switch to next input field or gizmo. |
| ↑ | Adjust value up or choose preceding item in a list. |

## Window shortcuts

| Key | Function |
| --- | --- |
| Alt+F4 | Close window. |
| Alt+spacebar | Display Control menu. |
| Ctrl+Shift+Tab | Switch to preceding pane. |
| Ctrl+Tab | Switch to next pane. |
| F6 | Switch between panes. |

## Windows desktop shortcuts

| Key | Function |
| --- | --- |
| Alt+Enter | Display selected item's Properties dialog box. |
| Alt+Esc | Cycle through open programs. |
| Alt+Shift+Tab | Switch to preceding program. |
| Alt+Tab | Switch to next program. |
| Application | Display shortcut menu for selected item. |
| Ctrl+Esc | Pop up Start button's menu. |
| F3 | Open the Search command. |
| Win | Pop up Start button's menu. |
| Win+Break | Display System Properties dialog box. |
| Win+D | Show the desktop (hide windows). |
| Win+E | Open Windows Explorer window. |
| Win+F | Open Search Companion (Find). |
| Win+L | Lock desktop. |
| Win+M | Minimize all windows. |
| Win+R | Display Run dialog box. |
| Win+Shift+M | Restore minimized windows. |
| Win+U | Open Utility Manager window. |

## Windows Explorer shortcuts

| Key | Function |
| --- | --- |
| Alt+Enter | Display selected item's Properties dialog box. |
| Backspace | Go up one level in folder hierarchy. |
| Ctrl+A | Select all files. |
| Ctrl+C | Copy selected file or files. |
| Ctrl+E | Open Search Companion. |
| Ctrl+H | Display History. |
| Ctrl+I | Display Favorites. |
| Ctrl+V | Paste cut or copied files. |
| Ctrl+X | Cut selected file or files for a move. |
| Delete | Delete file. |
| F2 | Rename file. |
| F5 | Refresh window contents. |
| Shift | When pressed, prevent inserted CD or DVD from playing automatically. |
| Shift+Delete | Permanently delete file. |

## Common application shortcuts

| Key | Function |
| --- | --- |
| Alt | Activate menu. |
| Ctrl+A | Select All. |
| Ctrl+B | Apply bold type. |
| Ctrl+C | Copy. |
| Ctrl+D | Unselect. |
| Ctrl+F4 | Close document window, but not program. |
| Ctrl+I | Apply italics. |
| Ctrl+N | Create new document. |
| Ctrl+O | Open. |
| Ctrl+P | Print. |
| Ctrl+S | Save. |
| Ctrl+U | Underline. |
| Ctrl+V | Paste. |

| Key | Function |
| --- | --- |
| Ctrl+W | Close window. |
| Ctrl+X | Cut. |
| Ctrl+Y | Redo. |
| Ctrl+Z | Undo. |
| Delete | Clear. |
| F10 | Activate menu. |

# Keyboard Types

There is really only one type of keyboard for the PC: the standard 104-key keyboard. It's called 104-key because it really does have 104 keys. That's three more keys than the old 101-key keyboard, which was a standard for about 15 years. (Before that, the original IBM PC used an 83-key keyboard.)

The extra three keys on the 104-key keyboard are the two Windows keys and the Application key. See also "Special Keys."

There are variations on the standard keyboard, including wireless keyboards, ergonomically designed keyboards, and keyboards with specialty buttons on them for doing things like sending e-mail, searching the Web, scanning documents, setting the speaker volume, and other tasks. Note that those keyboards and their special buttons are nonstandard.

# Keys for Editing Text

Windows uses a common set of keyboard commands to edit, change, or modify any text just about anywhere in Windows:

| Key | Function |
| --- | --- |
| ← | Move the text cursor left (back) one character. |
| → | Move the text cursor right (forward) one character. |
| ↑ | Move the text cursor up one line. |
| ↓ | Move the text cursor down one line. |
| Ctrl+← | Move the text cursor left one word. |
| Ctrl+→ | Move the text cursor right one word. |
| Home | Move the text cursor to the beginning of the line. |
| End | Move the text cursor to the end of the line. |

| Key | Function |
|-----|----------|
| Delete | Delete the character immediately to the right of the text cursor. |
| Backspace | Delete the character immediately preceding the text cursor. |
| PgUp | Move the text cursor up one screen. |
| PgDn | Move the text cursor down one screen. |
| Ctrl+PgUp | Move the text cursor up one full screen in the document. |
| Ctrl+PgDn | Move the text cursor down one full screen in the document. |
| Ctrl+↑ | Move the text cursor to the preceding paragraph. |
| Ctrl+↓ | Move the text cursor to the next paragraph. |
| Ctrl+Delete | Delete characters from the cursor's position to the end of the line. |
| Ctrl+End | Move the text cursor to the end of the document. |
| Ctrl+Home | Move the text cursor to the beginning of the document. |
| Insert | Insert characters in a line of text. Pressing the Insert button again types over the current text. |

# Names for Funky Keys

Symbols unusual abound on the PC keyboard — things that would mortify the standard eighth-grade typing teacher. Here are the common names for these unusual symbols:

| Symbol | Called |
|--------|--------|
| ! | Exclamation point, bang |
| # | Hash, pound sign |
| * | Asterisk, star, splat |
| . | Period, dot |
| / | Slash, forward slash |
| @ | At |
| [ ] | Square brackets |
| \ | Backslash |
| ^ | Circumflex, hat, control |
| _ | Underline, underscore |

| Symbol | Called |
|--------|--------|
| ` | Accent grave |
| { } | Curly brackets, braces |
| \| | Pipe, vertical bar |
| ~ | Tilde ("till-dee") |
| < > | Angle brackets, less-than greater-than |

# Setting the Repeat Delay and Repeat Rate

Yes, there is a Keyboard icon in the Control Panel. The icon doesn't do much, however, unlike the Mouse icon (see also Part XII). But it does let you control two important keyboard settings: the repeat delay and the repeat rate.

The *repeat delay* is the length of time the keyboard waits while you press a key before that key starts repeating. So, press and hold the D key, and eventually the computer repeats the letter: DDDDDD. The pause before it goes nuts like that is the repeat delay.

The *repeat rate* is how quickly the characters appear after the repeat delay time has elapsed.

 You use the Keyboard icon in the Control Panel to set the repeat delay and the repeat rate. There's a text box where you can check your settings before clicking the OK button to lock them in.

# Special Keys

A few keys carry more weight than others. These keys are important to know:

 **The Windows key:** This key is used primarily to pop up the Start button's menu, though the key can be used in combination with other keys to do various and interesting things. It's often abbreviated Win.

 **The Application key:** This key exists to the left of the second Windows key on the standard 104-key PC keyboard. This key is rarely used, though when you select an icon or item and press this key, that item's Properties dialog box is displayed. Yawn.

**The Fn key:** This key is found mostly on laptop PCs. It's used in combination with other keys on a laptop to produce key combinations not normally available on the smaller, laptop keyboard.

**The Enter key:** This key must be important because two of them are on the keyboard. Relax! Both Enter keys do the same thing. Enter is commonly used as a command key to signal to Windows that you're done typing a command or have finished making selections in a dialog box. It's also used when writing text to mark the end of a paragraph.

**The Tab key:** In Windows, you press Tab to move between fields in a dialog box. This is important to remember because pressing the Enter key is like clicking the OK button.

**The Esc key:** This key, also called *escape,* is used to cancel certain operations. It can also be used to close some windows.

**The Print Screen key:** This key is used to take a snapshot of the desktop (see also Part VIII). But, note that the key may also be labeled PrtSc or Pr Scr or some other cryptic combination. They're all Print Screen keys.

# The Mouse

Computers didn't always have mice, but back then computers weren't exactly that easy to use. You can thank all those graphics up on the screen for the necessity of a computer mouse. The mouse makes working with graphics — and even manipulating text — much easier. After all, computers don't live by keyboard input alone.

## In this part . . .

## *Basic Mouse Actions*

You can do only a few things with a computer mouse. Basically, you can roll it around and click the buttons. But doing that in various ways and in various combinations is given specific terms and jargon:

**Pointing:** The most basic mouse command is "point," as in "Point the mouse at the circle." This instruction requires you to move the mouse around on your desk, which controls the *mouse pointer* on the screen by moving it in a similar manner. You move and maneuver the mouse until the mouse pointer on the screen is pointing at some specific or interesting object.

**Clicking:** Pressing and releasing the mouse's button is known as clicking. But — aha! — the mouse has more than one button. Therefore, the plain click is a quick press (and release) of the mouse's main button, the one under your index finger. For right-handed people, that's the left mouse button.

Clicking the mouse is done in combination with pointing.

Clicking may also be done in combination with pressing a shift key on the keyboard: Shift, Ctrl, Alt, or a combination of these.

Clicking the mouse does indeed make a clicking noise. The computer may also be programmed to play a sound when you click the mouse, such as a squishing noise or painful little yelp.

**Right-clicking:** Pressing and releasing the right mouse button — the one not normally pressed — is a right-click. This is important to remember: A regular click is a click of the left button, and a right-click is specifically the right button.

**Double-click:** Two quick clicks in a row is a double-click. For example, a single click may merely select an object, to make it ready for manipulation. But a double-click does something more powerful, such as open an item or just cause it twice as much pain as a single click.

Double-clicking must be done quickly; if you take too long, the computer assumes that you have made two single clicks and not a double click. See also "Changing the Double-Click Rate."

There are also triple, quadruple, and quintuple clicks, depending on the program.

**Dragging:** The drag operation involves pointing the mouse at some object and then pressing and holding down the mouse's (left) button. You then move the mouse while keeping the button held down. Releasing the mouse button ends the drag operation.

Dragging is used to select groups of objects, an area, or a swath of text, or to move things around. The key is to keep the mouse button down.

**Selecting:** The mouse is often used to select an object or text on the screen. This is done by using a number of mouse techniques, depending on what is being selected.

For example, to select a graphical object or icon, you click the mouse on the object. That highlights the object, indicating that it's selected and ready for action.

To select a group of items or a span of text, you drag the mouse over the items or text. You can also select text by double-clicking the mouse on the text, or by triple-clicking or using a shift key while clicking. (It depends on the application.)

Selected objects and text appear highlighted on the screen.

The best way to get familiar with using the mouse is to play one of the many games included with Windows, such as Solitaire, FreeCell, or Minesweeper. These games help you practice the basic mouse movements just described, as well as kill some time and have fun.

# Changing the Double-Click Rate

A *double-click* is defined as two clicks in rapid succession at the same location. The location can vary slightly; the mouse programming forgives a few pixels on the screen one way or the other. But the "rapid succession" part can vary, and can be controlled:

*1.* Open the Control Panel.

*2.* Open the Mouse icon to display the Mouse Properties dialog box.

*3.* Click the Activities tab.

The tab may be different; because many types and brands of mice are available for computers, not every Mouse Properties dialog box is alike.

*4.* Use the slider in the Double-Click Speed area to adjust the double-click speed slower or faster. Test the speed by double-clicking the mouse in the Test Area display.

*5.* Click OK to set the new double-click speed.

# Connecting a Mouse

Connecting a mouse to the console is easy: Basically, you just plug the thing in.

For a mouse plugged into the console's mouse port, first turn off the console and then plug the mouse in. Turn the computer on after the mouse is connected. Likewise, turn off the console when you're disconnecting the mouse from the mouse port.

For USB and serial mice, you can connect or disconnect the mouse while keeping the console on.

Serial mice traditionally plug into the COM1 port. (COM2 is used internally by the dial-up modem.)

See also Part I.

# Extra Mouse Buttons

The standard PC mouse has three buttons:

- ✔ The left button, which is the main button
- ✔ The right button
- ✔ A center wheel, which is also a button

Some mice may have even more buttons. Windows doesn't officially use those buttons for anything, so you can use the Mouse icon in the Control Panel, on the Buttons tab, to assign functions to those extra buttons.

For example, the IntelliMouse Explorer has two bonus buttons on the left side, which can be manipulated with your right thumb. These buttons can be *mapped* to any key combination or assigned commands that do things in Windows. For this to work, you must install the specific software that comes with your computer mouse.

# Increasing the Mouse Pointer Visibility

It's easy to lose a mouse on the desktop. To help find the wayward little guy, you can activate some bonus pointer features:

*1.* Open the Control Panel.

*2.* Open the Mouse icon in the Control Panel to display the Mouse Properties dialog box.

3. Click the Pointer Options tab.

Several options are available to increase mouse visibility, depending on the type of mouse you have. The two common options are

- **Pointer Trails.** This option causes multiple pointers to "comet tail" after the mouse pointer.

- **Show Location.** This option causes a ring of concentric circles to appear around the pointer when either Ctrl key is pressed.

4. Make your selection, and then click OK.

You can also increase the pointer's size by choosing a larger pointer, or an animated pointer, or even an inverse color pointer. See also "Mouse Pointers."

## Left-Handed Mouse

Not everyone is right handed. There's hope for you southpaws, and for other folks who prefer to hold the mouse in their left hand. Windows lets you reassign the mouse buttons, left and right, so that you can use the right mouse button with your left hand — which makes sense and is quite a kind gesture to the left-handed part of the population:

1. Open the Control Panel.

2. Open the Mouse icon in the Control Panel to display the Mouse Properties dialog box.

3. Click the Buttons tab.

4. Change the function of the Left button to Right-Click.

Use the drop-down list to assign the new button function.

5. Change the function of the Right button to Click.

6. Click OK.

Remember that you have a left-handed mouse! Most computer documentation assumes that the mouse is right-handed. So whenever you see a "right-click" direction, remember to click your *left* mouse button.

# The Mouse Pad

A *mouse pad* is merely a small piece of foam rubber on which a computer mouse can roll very well. This is an optional item to purchase for a computer; in fact, optical mice don't need a mouse pad, although mechanical, or "ball," mice can really benefit from the textured surface a mouse pad offers.

Mouse pads are often covered in special designs or with pictures of something pleasing or inspiring.

Just about anything can be used as a mouse pad, but textured surfaces work best. Avoid slick mouse pads.

A mouse pad also ensures that you will have at least one clean area on your desk to roll the mouse around!

# Mouse Pointers

The graphical doohickey that the mouse manipulates on the desktop is the *mouse pointer.* Some may call it a *mouse cursor* or just *cursor,* but that's easy to confuse with the text cursor. To avoid confusion, and because the thing looks like a pointer anyway, I use the term mouse pointer.

## Making the pointer go faster or slower

The mouse pointer can be geared to go faster or slower, which is controlled from the Mouse Properties dialog box, on the Pointer Options tab:

1. Open the Control Panel.

2. Open the Mouse icon in the Control Panel to display the Mouse Properties dialog box.

3. Click the Pointer Options tab.

4. Adjust the pointer speed slider slower or faster.

5. Click OK.

A faster pointer is easier to use when you have a larger screen or high screen-size setting. Slower pointers are better when you're working with graphics or other things that require precise mouse movement.

If the Mouse Properties dialog box sports an acceleration option for the mouse pointer, I highly recommend that you use it. The acceleration option directs the pointer to move in greater distances when you move the mouse faster and to move the pointer more precisely when the mouse is moving slowly.

## Choosing a new pointer

The mouse pointer can be replaced with just about any graphical image, from a real arrow to a pointing hand to a tomahawk. This is done by using the Pointers tab in the Mouse Properties dialog box:

1. Open the Control Panel.

2. Open the Mouse icon in the Control Panel to display the Mouse Properties dialog box.

3. Click the Pointers tab.

4. In the scrolling list of pointers, click to select the Normal Select pointer.

5. Click the Browse button.

   A special type of Open dialog box appears, listing a cartload of various pointers available in Windows. Notice the special preview area in the lower-left corner of this dialog box.

6. Click to select a new pointer from the many options listed.

   The files beginning with the name `arrow` are all pointing arrows, though you're not limited to that selection for replacing the Normal Select pointer.

7. Click the Open button to choose the highlighted pointer.

8. Click OK.

You can use these steps to replace any of the various mouse pointers. Note that there are different pointers for different activities. There are no rules for what is or isn't a proper pointer — but keep in mind that all Windows documentation assumes that you're using the standard set of pointers.

Yes, it's okay to have fun here.

## Using an animated pointer

Many of the optional mouse pointers are animated. For example, you can use spinning barber polls, lumbering dinosaurs, and snapping fingers. To select one of these animated cursors, after Step 5 in the preceding subsection, choose Animated Cursors (*.ani) from the Files of Type drop-down list in the Browse dialog box.

## Loading a set of pointers

Windows comes with preset groups, or themes, of mouse pointers. You can choose one of these themes by using the Scheme drop-down list at the top of the Pointers tab in the Mouse Properties dialog box. By choosing a theme or scheme, you can quickly replace the whole set of mouse pointers at one time.

### Saving your own set of pointers

After customizing your mouse pointers, you can save your collection as a scheme, which saves time in case you need to reset all the mouse pointers at some later point. To save a scheme on the Pointers tab of the Mouse Properties dialog box, first set each individual mouse pointer, and then click the Save As button. Use the Save As dialog box to save your scheme just as you would save any file.

I have a whole collection of personal schemes. For them, I created a My Schemes folder inside my My Documents folder.

## Mouse Types

There is really no such thing as a standard PC mouse. All mice have left and right buttons, and most of them now have a wheel button or similar gizmo between the buttons. But that's where the similarities stop.

This section covers various mouse options. Some mice may have most or all of the options, and some may have none. The variety is endless.

### Air mouse

The very peculiar *air* mouse can be held up, off the desktop. In a way, it kind of works like a TV remote control. That's good for demonstrations and perhaps some games, but, otherwise, mice work best next to the keyboard, where they remain handy and accessible.

### Mechanical, or ball, mouse

The traditional computer mouse uses a round ball on its underside to detect movement. In fact, the very first mouse, pioneered in the 1960s, used such a ball to detect movement, though today the balls (and the mouse) are much smaller. This type of mouse is known as a *mechanical* mouse.

### Optical mouse

The *optical* mouse uses a special light sensor to detect movement. This mouse has, aside from the buttons, no moving parts, which makes it extremely reliable. Also, unlike the mechanical mouse, the optical mouse doesn't require a mouse pad or textured surface — though it doesn't work on smooth, reflective surfaces.

### Trackball mouse

The *trackball* is often called the upside-down mouse. With a trackball, the mouse is stationary and the mouse pointer is moved by rotating a large ball atop the mouse with your fingers. The mouse also sports buttons and, often, a *scroll ring* around the ball, used like the wheel button on a regular mouse.

## Wheel button

The *wheel button* mouse has a wheel, or scroll, button between its two regular buttons. The wheel can be clicked, just like a regular button, and it's known as a *wheel-click.*

The wheel button can also be pressed and held, which on most wheel mice lets the mouse pan or scan the document, by scrolling it up, down, left, or right or in whatever direction the mouse is being dragged.

The wheel is primarily rolled back or forth, which has the effect of scrolling the contents of whatever window the mouse is pointing at — similar to using the up or down arrows on the keyboard. In fact, the amount of scroll can be adjusted in the wheel mouse's Properties dialog box.

In some applications, pressing the Ctrl key on the keyboard while scrolling the wheel button zooms in or out on the document.

The latest rage in computer mouse wheels is the tilting wheel: You can tilt the wheel to the left or right to pan a long document left or right.

## Wireless mouse

A *wireless* mouse requires no wires to connect to the desktop, which is great if you have a cluttered desk already. There are two types of wireless mice:

- **Radio frequency (RF):** This mouse uses an electronic signal to connect to the base station.

- **Infrared (IR):** This mouse uses an infrared light to connect to the base station. The path between the mouse and base station must not be obscured or else the IR mouse doesn't work.

Wireless mice require batteries, which I recommend that you keep on hand in abundance. Either that, or the mouse must be recharged. I recommend getting a rechargeable mouse base station, which not only keeps the wireless mouse in a convenient place, but also recharges the mouse when it's docked.

Eventually, wires come into play with wireless mice. The base station, or receiving unit, must be connected to the console somehow, either directly to the mouse port or into a USB port.

# Glossary: Tech Talk

AGP: Acronym for Accelerated Graphics Port, a special type of expansion slot into which you can plug special high-speed video adapters. Unlike other types of expansion slots, AGP allows video cards to "speak" directly with the computer's microprocessor.

All Programs menu: The main program menu branching from the Start button's menu. Pretty much every program installed on your computer appears somewhere on the All Programs menu or on one of its ubiquitous submenus.

Alt: A special shift key on the PC keyboard, often used in combination with some other key, though it can be used by itself.

application: Another name for a computer program, though usually describing a major software category, such as word processing, spreadsheet, or e-mail.

Apply button: Used like the OK button in a dialog box, in that it accepts any changes. Unlike clicking the OK button, clicking the Apply button doesn't close the dialog box.

arrow keys: Another term for the cursor keys on the keyboard. There are four basic arrow keys: up, down, left, and right.

asterisk: The * symbol on the keyboard. Used to represent multiplication in many programs. Also, the multiple-character filename wildcard.

background: 1. A multitasking term indicating a program that is running a task you aren't currently working with or don't have visible on the screen. Most printing takes place in the background. 2. An image on the desktop, also known as wallpaper.

backspace: 1. The key on the keyboard that has the word *Backspace* on it. This key might also have a left-pointing arrow on it. 2. To press the Backspace key, which deletes something. In a word processor, the Backspace key erases the character immediately to the left of the cursor.

BIOS: Acronym for Basic Input/Output System, the chip responsible for the vital communications inside a computer or between the computer and a specific device. Several BIOS chips are inside a PC. Collectively, they comprise the chipset, or the basic computer hardware on the motherboard.

bold: In word processing or desktop publishing, the attribute applied to text that **darkens** it.

boot: 1. To start a computer. 2. To load a specific operating system.

boot disk: The disk used to start your computer. Most often, the boot disk is the hard drive, though you can start a computer with a floppy, CD, or DVD.

broadband: Another term for a high-speed Internet connection. Broadband can be DSL, cable, satellite, or some other zippy form of access.

bug: A problem that prevents a program from working properly. Typically unexpected, bugs are something that nearly every program has.

burn: To write information to a CD, either data or music. This is the final step in using the CD-R or CD-RW disc.

button: Either a physical button on the keyboard or console or the graphical representation of a button appearing on the screen. You "press" graphical buttons by using the mouse.

byte: A single storage location, either in computer memory or on disk. A byte can store one character of information.

cable: A wire or bundle of wires used to connect things inside or outside of a computer.

cable modem: The fastest type of modem. However, you must live in an area where a cable company offers cable modem access.

Cancel button: Used to dismiss a dialog box and ignore any changes that were made. Pressing the Esc key is the same as clicking the Cancel button.

CD-R: A CD that can have information written to it. The R stands for *r*ecordable.

CD-ROM: Acronym for Compact Disc–Read-Only Memory. CD-ROMs are discs that contain megabytes of information.

CD-RW: A CD that can have information written to it, and can also be erased and used again. RW stands for *r*ewriteable.

Celeron: Another popular type of microprocessor for the PC; similar to the Pentium but not as powerful or as expensive.

central processing unit (CPU): The computer's microprocessor. Often used incorrectly to refer to the console.

character: Any letter, number, or symbol. Most keys on a PC's keyboard are adorned with characters, which are displayed on the screen when the keys are pressed.

child folder: Another name for a subfolder, but specifically with reference to the containing folder. For example, any folder inside the My Documents folder is a child folder of the My Documents folder.

chipset: A collection of circuits used together inside a PC for basic functions or to provide basic hardware, such as graphics or networking.

clear: To erase or delete.

clipboard: A temporary storage area for items that have been cut or copied using the Edit⇨Cut or Edit⇨Copy command. The Edit⇨Paste command is used to dump the clipboard's contents into the appropriate location or program. The clipboard can hold only one item at a time.

close: To remove a window from the screen or a document from an application's window. Can also mean to exit a program.

connector: One end of a computer cable; matches a plug-in or hole on the console or computer peripheral to which it attaches.

console: The main computer box; the thing that all other parts of your computer plug into. Sometimes mistakenly referred to as the CPU.

Control Panel: The place to go to customize various aspects of Windows and your PC.

CRT monitor: The traditional glass-screen computer monitor. CRT stands for *cathode ray tube*, the doodad inside the monitor that displays the image.

Ctrl: A special shift key, called Control, on the PC's keyboard. This key is often used in combination with other keys to carry out commands or do other cool things.

cursor: A blinking underline, block, or vertical line on the screen that shows where new text appears in a window or document. Also mistakenly used to refer to the mouse pointer. *Cursor* is from the Latin word for *runner*.

cursor keys: Another term for the arrow keys on the keyboard. The keys are called cursor keys because they manipulate the cursor. Unlike the arrow keys, cursor keys also include Insert, Delete, Home, End, Page Up, and Page Down.

data: The computer term for organized stuff or information.

default: An ugly word meaning "the setting selected for you when you don't make any other choice." For example, the default printer is the printer Windows chooses to use when you don't specify a printer.

delete: To remove a file from a disk; to erase or kill the file or a chunk of text or any selected thingy.

desktop: The main screen displayed by Windows. The desktop is home to various icons, the taskbar, the Start button, plus an optional pretty picture.

DIMM: Acronym for Dual In-line Memory Module, a small expansion card on which memory chips are placed.

disk: The part of the disk drive on which information is written. It can be a removable disk, such as a floppy disk or CD, or a nonremovable disk, such as the disk inside a hard drive.

display: The monitor or computer screen — specifically, the information shown on the screen.

double-click: To press the left (or primary) mouse button twice in rapid succession without moving the mouse between clicks.

drag: To move an onscreen object with the mouse. Also, for a man to dress in women's clothing.

drive: A disk drive in the computer system, usually described by the type of drive it is: CD-ROM drive or flash memory drive, for example.

driver: The software program that controls some piece of hardware. For example, a printer driver is used to control how the printer prints information. There are modem drivers, graphics display drivers, network drivers, women drivers, and more.

DSL modem: A type of high-speed modem used with a phone company's DSL, or Digital Subscriber Line, connection.

DVD: Acronym for Digital Versatile (or Video) Disc, a high-capacity form of read-only computer storage. A DVD disc can store as much as 4.7 gigabytes of information per side.

DVD recordable: One of several types of DVD disc used to record information. The variety includes DVD-R, DVD+R, DVD-RW, DVD+RW, DVD-RAM, and probably a few others that I don't really care to write about just now.

eject: To remove a disk from a disk drive.

Enter key: A special key on the keyboard used to end input or a paragraph of text, or as a substitute for clicking the OK button in a dialog box. The PC keyboard has two Enter keys, one in the typewriter key area and the second on the numeric keypad. Both Enter keys work the same.

erase: To remove a file from a disk.

error message: A cryptic note the computer displays to let you know that the program isn't working right or that you've screwed up.

Ethernet: The type of networking system PCs use.

expansion card: A circuit board that plugs into expansion slots on the motherboard and is used to add new features to your PC.

expansion slot: A slot into which expansion cards are plugged, on the PC's motherboard. There are three types of expansion slots: AGP, ISA, and PCI.

file: The basic chunk of information stored on a computer disk. Files can be programs, text, raw data, graphics, or other stuff.

fixed disk: Another term for a hard drive. The disk is "fixed," as in *not removable,* not as in *repaired.*

F-key: A function key.

floppy disk: A removable disk, traditional for PCs but rarely used these days because their capacity is too low to hold today's larger files.

floppy drive: A disk drive designed to read from and write to floppy disks.

folder: A container for files as well as other folders. Folders are used to help organize the information you collect or create on your computer.

font: A collection of characters with predefined sizes and styles. Most word processors and desktop publishing programs let you choose different fonts to make your writing prettier.

function keys: The keys labeled F1 through F12 on your keyboard. Each key does a specific thing or can be programmed to do certain things.

gigabyte (GB, B): One billion bytes, or 1,000 megabytes. Used to measure computer storage, usually hard drive storage.

glitch: A problem (sometimes temporary) that causes a program to work erratically or not at all.

graphics: Artwork; anything nontext on a computer.

hard copy: Printed information.

hard disk: The physical disk used to store information inside a hard drive. The thing you use in a computer is the *hard drive;* hard disk is a technical term.

hard drive: The main device for long-term storage in a PC.

hardware: The physical part of a computer; anything you can touch and see.

Help system: The program used to display (helpful) information in Windows.

icon: A tiny picture used to represent something else, such as an image used to represent a file on disk.

ink cartridge: The small container used to supply inkjet printers with ink. Different cartridges have different colors of ink, or sometimes multiple colors are put in separate compartments of single ink cartridges.

inkjet printer: A type of printer that sprays ink on paper rather than smacks an inked ribbon against the page, as an impact printer does. Inkjet printers are quieter than dot-matrix printers, and produce better-quality printing (but not as good as laser printers).

insertion pointer: The cursor, on the screen, used in a program to mark where new text appears.

IP: Acronym for Internet Protocol, a set of rules for sending and receiving information over a network as well as over the Internet (which is just a big network anyway).

IP address: An ID number given to computers on the network according to various rules and protocols. IP stands for Internet Protocol. The IP address is a group of four numbers, each from 0 to 255, separated by dots, as in 192.168.0.1.

ISA: Acronym for Industry Standard Architecture, the name given to the traditional, old-fashioned expansion slots found inside PCs. These slots are kept around for compatibility reasons.

italic: In word processing or desktop publishing, the attribute applied to text that *slants* it — like the leaning tower of Pisa in Italy!

jack: Another term for a hole or connector on the console, into which cables plug for connecting external devices.

key: A button on the keyboard.

keyboard: The device you use to communicate with the computer. You mostly interact with the computer by typing on the keyboard.

keyboard shortcut: A single key or combination of keys that activates a command. Specifically, this term refers to the shortcut shown on a menu, such as Ctrl+V, the keyboard shortcut for pasting something from the clipboard into a document.

kilobyte (KB, K): One thousand bytes of storage, either on disk or in RAM. It's exactly 1,024 bytes, but who really cares?

Landscape mode: Printing that goes the long way on a sheet of paper — wide instead of narrow.

laptop: A computer small enough to fit on your lap without crushing your kneecaps.

laser printer: A type of printer that uses a laser beam to generate an image and electronically transfer it to paper.

LCD monitor: The thin, flat-screen monitor used with a laptop; now trendy to have with a desktop computer.

MAC address: The physical address, or serial number, given to the networking hardware in your PC. The MAC address is often used for security purposes when networking — specifically, wireless networking.

map: To assign a drive letter to a folder or a shared disk drive or folder on the network.

Maximize button: The button in the upper-right corner of a window that is used to make the window fill the entire screen.

megabyte (MB, M): Approximately 1 million bytes of computer storage.

memory: Information storage inside a computer — specifically, RAM.

menu: A list of commands or options available within a program. Menus show you options on a list.

microprocessor: The main processing chip inside a computer, specifically dwelling in the console. Also called the CPU or just "the processor."

Minimize button: Used to turn an open window into a button on the taskbar. The Minimize button is located in the upper-right corner of the window.

minitower PC: A type of computer that sits tall and squat, usually on top of the desktop but often beneath.

modem: The device that enables your computer to connect to other computers using standard phone lines. Today, modems are used primarily to connect with the Internet.

monitor: Another name for the display. It's that thing you stare into for hours on end when using your computer.

motherboard: The main circuit board of a computer, located inside the console.

mount: To add a disk drive to your computer system. Windows does this automatically whenever you insert a removable disk.

mouse: A pointing device used to provide input as well as to manipulate graphical objects on the screen.

mouse pointer: The graphical representation of the mouse on the screen, usually a pointing arrow. The mouse pointer, manipulated by using the mouse, mimics the mouse's movements on the desktop.

My Computer: An icon representing the contents of your PC in Windows — all the disk drives, printers, plus other folders.

My Documents: A folder window used as the primary location for where you save stuff on your computer.

network: A system of computers connected to each other for sharing information and computer resources, such as hard drives and printers.

networking: Connecting two or more computers to share resources, such as disk drives, printers, and high-speed modems.

NIC: Acronym for *n*etwork *i*nformation *c*ard (also known as an Ethernet card), the adapter or circuitry on the motherboard responsible for networking in a PC.

Notepad: The text editor program that comes with Windows.

notification area: Another term for the *system tray*.

numeric keypad: The portion of the keyboard that contains the number keys, usually all grouped into rows and columns by themselves.

online: Another way of saying that two devices are connected, such as the modem connected to the Internet.

open: To access a program or file, just as you would open a book if you wanted to read it.

operating system: The main program that controls the PC hardware, runs your programs, and interacts with you to help control the computer.

parent folder: A folder in which a subfolder dwells. The parent folder is one level up in the folder hierarchy.

pathname: The full name of a file. The pathname includes the drive where the file lives, the folders in which the file is saved, and then the file itself. The drive letter is followed by a colon and a backslash that separate the folder names: for example, C:\My Documents\kids\Jordan\2006.

PC: Acronym for personal computer — specifically, a computer designed to run the Windows operating system.

PCI: Acronym for Peripheral Component Interconnect, a type of expansion slot on the PC's motherboard.

Pentium: The name given to the popular line of PC microprocessors developed by Intel.

playlist: A collection of songs or other music in Windows Media Player. Only playlists can be burned to create musical CDs.

Portrait mode: The tall mode, versus the wide mode for a rectangular image or sheet of paper. Normally, the printer prints on paper in Portrait mode. The other mode is called *Landscape* mode.

power strip: A device containing several power sockets, designed like an extension cord and used to plug in myriad devices surrounding your computer.

printer: A device for putting information on paper.

RAM: Acronym for Random-Access Memory, the computer's memory or primary form of temporary storage.

resources: Something that is used by a computer; a necessary component or vital piece of equipment. Examples of resources are memory (RAM), disk storage, and the printer.

Restore button: A button used to reposition a window to its previous size and location after the window has been maximized or minimized. This button appears in the upper-right corner of the window.

ROM: Acronym for Read-Only Memory, a type of computer memory that cannot be erased. Normally, only computer instructions for the hardware are stored in ROM.

satellite modem: One of the fastest modems available. You combine an outdoor antenna and a subscription to a satellite service.

save: To store data in a permanent form, such as a file on a disk drive.

screen: Another term for the computer monitor; specifically, the front part of the monitor where information is displayed.

screen saver: A special program that periodically blanks out the screen and replaces it with utter darkness or often some form of graphical or entertaining images.

shared: A disk drive or printer that is available for use by other computers on the network.

Shift key: A modifier key used primarily to produce uppercase letters on the keyboard, or used in combination with other keys to do amazing things.

software: The brains of the computer. Software tells the hardware what to do.

SSID: Acronym for Service Set Identifier, a special code used in wireless networking; also, slang for the name of the wireless network.

Start button: The big button! The Start button lives on the taskbar and is used to start a number of activities in Windows. Clicking the Start button displays the Start menu and various options or places to go.

Start menu: The main menu in Windows; displays locations, important and recently opened programs, help information, other commands, and the All Programs menu.

subdirectory: An older term for a subfolder.

subfolder: A folder inside another folder.

submenu: A menu that appears after you choose an item from the primary menu.

surge suppressor: A special type of power strip that helps fight irregularities in the electrical supply. It's more expensive than a plain power strip.

system tray: The location on the taskbar for a group of tiny icons, the time, and the volume control. Also referred to as the *notification area.*

taskbar: One of the main Windows components, with the Start button on one end and the system tray on the other, plus buttons representing open windows and programs in the middle. The taskbar can also be home to various toolbars.

terabyte (TB, T): A huge amount of computer storage; 1 trillion bytes or 1,000 gigabytes or 1 million megabytes.

text: Stuff you've typed into a document. Letters, numbers, and other characters or symbols on your keyboard create text.

toner cartridge: The source of ink for a laser printer.

toolbar: A collection of buttons, plus other tools and gizmos. A toolbar is often a long, skinny palette that holds those buttons and controls. Toolbars are found in programs, and some even dwell on the taskbar.

tower PC: A desktop computer on its side, but really a computer that was made to stand vertically (up and down). These computers have more room and tend to be more powerful than mere mortal desktop models.

undelete: To put something back the way it was before you deleted it.

underline: In word processing or desktop publishing, the attribute applied to text that makes it look like it has a line under it.

undo: To retract the last action you did, whether it was adding or deleting text or applying bold or italics.

unmount: To remove or eject a disk from a computer system. To unmount the disk is to remove it from the file system, which also ensures that the files on the disk are no longer in use.

UPS: Acronym for uninterruptible power supply, a standby power device used to keep the computer running during brief power outages, or to give you enough time to shut it down during power outages.

utility: A category of software that includes tools and programs specifically designed to fix, diagnose, automate, or do other amazing things in a computer. Unlike applications, utilities don't help you create things on the computer.

wallpaper: An older term for the background image on the desktop.

window: An area on the screen that displays data, programs, or information. A window can be moved, resized, opened, and closed, allowing you to organize the data on your computer screen.

Windows: An operating system, currently the most common one used to control a PC. The current version of Windows is XP. Windows XP has two versions: Home and Professional.

wireless networking: Connecting to a network without a physical connection. With wireless networking, the network information is sent and received using radio signals.

writeable folder: A preparatory folder in which files waiting to be copied to a CD-R/RW are kept until the disc is burned.

zoom: To enlarge or reduce an image — typically, a document displayed in a window.

# Notes

# Notes

# Notes

## USINESS, CAREERS & PERSONAL FINANCE

*rant Writing* DUMMIES

*Home Buying* DUMMIES

-7645-5307-0    0-7645-5331-3 *†

**Also available:**

- Accounting For Dummies †
  0-7645-5314-3
- Business Plans Kit For Dummies †
  0-7645-5365-8
- Cover Letters For Dummies
  0-7645-5224-4
- Frugal Living For Dummies
  0-7645-5403-4
- Leadership For Dummies
  0-7645-5176-0
- Managing For Dummies
  0-7645-1771-6

- Marketing For Dummies
  0-7645-5600-2
- Personal Finance For Dummies *
  0-7645-2590-5
- Project Management
  For Dummies
  0-7645-5283-X
- Resumes For Dummies †
  0-7645-5471-9
- Selling For Dummies
  0-7645-5363-1
- Small Business Kit For Dummies *†
  0-7645-5093-4

## OME & BUSINESS COMPUTER BASICS

*Windows XP* DUMMIES

*Excel 2003* DUMMIES

-7645-4074-2    0-7645-3758-X

**Also available:**

- ACT! 6 For Dummies
  0-7645-2645-6
- iLife '04 All-in-One Desk Reference
  For Dummies
  0-7645-7347-0
- iPAQ For Dummies
  0-7645-6769-1
- Mac OS X Panther Timesaving
  Techniques For Dummies
  0-7645-5812-9
- Macs For Dummies
  0-7645-5656-8
- Microsoft Money 2004 For Dummies
  0-7645-4195-1

- Office 2003 All-in-One Desk
  Reference For Dummies
  0-7645-3883-7
- Outlook 2003 For Dummies
  0-7645-3759-8
- PCs For Dummies
  0-7645-4074-2
- TiVo For Dummies
  0-7645-6923-6
- Upgrading and Fixing PCs
  For Dummies
  0-7645-1665-5
- Windows XP Timesaving
  Techniques For Dummies
  0-7645-3748-2

## OOD, HOME, GARDEN, HOBBIES, MUSIC & PETS

*Feng Shui* DUMMIES

*Poker* DUMMIES

-7645-5295-3    0-7645-5232-5

**Also available:**

- Bass Guitar For Dummies
  0-7645-2487-9
- Diabetes Cookbook For Dummies
  0-7645-5230-9
- Gardening For Dummies *
  0-7645-5130-2
- Guitar For Dummies
  0-7645-5106-X
- Holiday Decorating For Dummies
  0-7645-2570-0
- Home Improvement All-in-One
  For Dummies
  0-7645-5680-0

- Knitting For Dummies
  0-7645-5395-X
- Piano For Dummies
  0-7645-5105-1
- Puppies For Dummies
  0-7645-5255-4
- Scrapbooking For Dummies
  0-7645-7208-3
- Senior Dogs For Dummies
  0-7645-5818-8
- Singing For Dummies
  0-7645-2475-5
- 30-Minute Meals For Dummies
  0-7645-2589-1

## TERNET & DIGITAL MEDIA

*Digital Photography* DUMMIES

*Starting an eBay Business* DUMMIES

-7645-1664-7    0-7645-6924-4

**Also available:**

- 2005 Online Shopping Directory
  For Dummies
  0-7645-7495-7
- CD & DVD Recording For Dummies
  0-7645-5956-7
- eBay For Dummies
  0-7645-5654-1
- Fighting Spam For Dummies
  0-7645-5965-6
- Genealogy Online For Dummies
  0-7645-5964-8
- Google For Dummies
  0-7645-4420-9

- Home Recording For Musicians
  For Dummies
  0-7645-1634-5
- The Internet For Dummies
  0-7645-4173-0
- iPod & iTunes For Dummies
  0-7645-7772-7
- Preventing Identity Theft
  For Dummies
  0-7645-7336-5
- Pro Tools All-in-One Desk
  Reference For Dummies
  0-7645-5714-9
- Roxio Easy Media Creator
  For Dummies
  0-7645-7131-1

eparate Canadian edition also available
eparate U.K. edition also available

ailable wherever books are sold. For more information or to order direct: U.S. customers
t www.dummies.com or call 1-877-762-2974.
. customers visit www.wileyeurope.com or call 0800 243407. Canadian customers visit
w.wiley.ca or call 1-800-567-4797.

## SPORTS, FITNESS, PARENTING, RELIGION & SPIRITUALITY

0-7645-5146-9

0-7645-5418-2

**Also available:**
- Adoption For Dummies
  0-7645-5488-3
- Basketball For Dummies
  0-7645-5248-1
- The Bible For Dummies
  0-7645-5296-1
- Buddhism For Dummies
  0-7645-5359-3
- Catholicism For Dummies
  0-7645-5391-7
- Hockey For Dummies
  0-7645-5228-7

- Judaism For Dummies
  0-7645-5299-6
- Martial Arts For Dummies
  0-7645-5358-5
- Pilates For Dummies
  0-7645-5397-6
- Religion For Dummies
  0-7645-5264-3
- Teaching Kids to Read
  For Dummies
  0-7645-4043-2
- Weight Training For Dummies
  0-7645-5168-X
- Yoga For Dummies
  0-7645-5117-5

## TRAVEL

0-7645-5438-7

0-7645-5453-0

**Also available:**
- Alaska For Dummies
  0-7645-1761-9
- Arizona For Dummies
  0-7645-6938-4
- Cancún and the Yucatán
  For Dummies
  0-7645-2437-2
- Cruise Vacations For Dummies
  0-7645-6941-4
- Europe For Dummies
  0-7645-5456-5
- Ireland For Dummies
  0-7645-5455-7

- Las Vegas For Dummies
  0-7645-5448-4
- London For Dummies
  0-7645-4277-X
- New York City For Dummies
  0-7645-6945-7
- Paris For Dummies
  0-7645-5494-8
- RV Vacations For Dummies
  0-7645-5443-3
- Walt Disney World & Orlando
  For Dummies
  0-7645-6943-0

## GRAPHICS, DESIGN & WEB DEVELOPMENT

0-7645-4345-8

0-7645-5589-8

**Also available:**
- Adobe Acrobat 6 PDF
  For Dummies
  0-7645-3760-1
- Building a Web Site For Dummies
  0-7645-7144-3
- Dreamweaver MX 2004
  For Dummies
  0-7645-4342-3
- FrontPage 2003 For Dummies
  0-7645-3882-9
- HTML 4 For Dummies
  0-7645-1995-6
- Illustrator CS For Dummies
  0-7645-4084-X

- Macromedia Flash MX 2004
  For Dummies
  0-7645-4358-X
- Photoshop 7 All-in-One Desk
  Reference For Dummies
  0-7645-1667-1
- Photoshop CS Timesaving
  Techniques For Dummies
  0-7645-6782-9
- PHP 5 For Dummies
  0-7645-4166-8
- PowerPoint 2003 For Dummies
  0-7645-3908-6
- QuarkXPress 6 For Dummies
  0-7645-2593-X

## NETWORKING, SECURITY, PROGRAMMING & DATABASES

0-7645-6852-3

0-7645-5784-X

**Also available:**
- A+ Certification For Dummies
  0-7645-4187-0
- Access 2003 All-in-One Desk
  Reference For Dummies
  0-7645-3988-4
- Beginning Programming
  For Dummies
  0-7645-4997-9
- C For Dummies
  0-7645-7068-4
- Firewalls For Dummies
  0-7645-4048-3
- Home Networking For Dummies
  0-7645-42796

- Network Security For Dummies
  0-7645-1679-5
- Networking For Dummies
  0-7645-1677-9
- TCP/IP For Dummies
  0-7645-1760-0
- VBA For Dummies
  0-7645-3989-2
- Wireless All In-One Desk Reference
  For Dummies
  0-7645-7496-5
- Wireless Home Networking
  For Dummies
  0-7645-3910-8

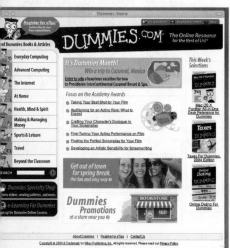